Speaking the Truth in Love

Speaking the Truth in Love

How to Be an Assertive Christian

Ruth N. Koch
Kenneth C. Haugk

Stephen Ministries • St. Louis, Missouri

Contents

Part Five: The Assertive, Loving Christian

Appendixes

Introduction:
Read This Book Assertively!

As you read this book, participate in it. Be active. Assimilate. Supply your own personal examples as you read. Take hold of the material. Wrestle with it, apply it to your own life, test it, challenge it, discuss it. Involve yourself in this book.

A good way to begin is to use the "Assertiveness Inventory" in appendix A. Since all people behave passively, aggressively, or assertively at some times and in some situations, this inventory can help you determine when and where you are most likely to be passive, aggressive, or assertive. Using the inventory can guide you to areas in your personal life and relationships where this book might help you grow.

Three Fundamental Principles

Three fundamental principles underlie this book: that individuals are response-able, that people continually make choices, and that God will direct you as you learn to think and behave assertively.

Individuals Are Response-Able

Individuals have a God-given ability to respond to life. We are not inert lumps of clay; each of us has a mind and a spirit capable of responding to God, to self, and to other people. We are alive, we are open, we are capable of interaction. We can try ideas on for size, we can experiment with new behaviors, we can test our own thoughts and perceptions as we bump up against the thoughts and perceptions of others. We can change our behavior, revise our thoughts, and understand ideas in new ways. We have the ability to respond to God, to ideas, to others. We have the ability to respond to life!

People Continually Make Choices

Some choices are as obvious as whether to take a new job and move to a new community or whether to choose pork chops or chicken for dinner.

Other choices are not as apparent and may not seem like choices at all. A person who'd like to offer a sincere compliment may feel so embarrassed and tongue-tied that he stands silently, wishing he could move toward the other person and say what he thinks. Another person may choose to keep an opinion to herself during a discussion among friends, perhaps saying to herself, "My opinion doesn't carry much weight anyway." Sometimes people make a choice *not* to choose; when they do, they are choosing the status quo and its consequences, whatever they may be.

Because all of us make choices of great and small significance every day, it's important to realize that you are indeed making choices. And, because some of your choices may surprise and puzzle you, you need to begin to understand some of the reasons for those particular choices.

To discover some of the reasons for your choices and therefore to develop increased self-awareness, you can ask yourself certain questions: What has been my experience in a similar situation? What choices did I make then, and was the outcome what I expected? What do I expect to happen this time as a result of my choice?

The goal of developing your self-awareness is that you begin to make an increasing number of choices consciously and deliberately. Your choices then will reflect your growing awareness of God's will for your life, your own self-knowledge, and your awareness of the needs of others.

God Will Direct You As You Learn to Think and Behave Assertively

If you're willing to turn your learning process over to God, God will move you in a life-giving direction. God will show you how to maintain your Christian integrity as you follow the model and direction of Scripture in learning to think and behave assertively. Making the decision to submit to God's leading as you learn about assertiveness is in itself an assertive act.

Learning new ways of acting and thinking might stir up all kinds of fear in you. Most people will admit to being wary of newness, cautious in the face of change. Your possible concern about learning to be an assertive Christian is no exception. While new ideas may excite and stimulate you, you are also likely to be experiencing some anxiety and fear. Here are six questions that might trouble Christians when they think about becoming more assertive, along with the reasons why you don't have to worry about them.

Six Questions You Don't Have to Worry About

1. Will becoming assertive make me rude and bossy and cause me to lose all my friends?

If you weren't rude and bossy before you learned assertiveness, you won't suddenly become rude and bossy after you become more assertive. In fact, you may well notice a pleasant change in your friendships brought about by your enhanced self-confidence and newfound ability to express your own preferences and to honor the choices of others.

Your friends will enjoy you as a genuinely assertive person who participates actively in the friendship-building process by revealing your own needs and caring about your friends' needs.

2. Will becoming assertive make me obnoxious, power-seeking, aggressive, and domineering?

Whew! Rest easy on that one. Learning to be assertive will actually reduce any aggressive or dominating behaviors you might have because you will learn how to better express your own needs without giving offense or having to make a show of power. The genuinely assertive person is genuinely respectful of others.

3. *Will becoming assertive compromise my Christian sense of servanthood?*

For Christians who sincerely desire to follow God's example of selfless service and sacrifice, this is an understandable fear. You may be relieved to know that Jesus himself provided an excellent example of assertive living as he made choices and dealt with individuals in a way that didn't compromise his purpose and ministry, his goals and personal needs. At the same time, he sacrificially focused on the ultimate good of others. The genuinely assertive person makes choices and adopts behaviors that reflect that person's God-pleasing values and spiritual foundations.

4. *Will becoming assertive make me a selfish, self-centered, self-serving person, always out to get my own way?*

Actually, learning assertion skills will probably enhance your ability to give selfless attention and genuine care to others. Learning clear-cut, straightforward ways to have your own needs met and to speak up when it is appropriate to do so allows you to give up some of the old manipulative, indirect, calculating methods you might sometimes have used to get your way and to get your own needs met. Genuinely assertive people are responsive to their own needs, and that frees them to attend to the needs of others.

5. *Will becoming assertive mean I will start saying no all the time when I actually enjoy saying yes to projects and people at times?*

Assertive behavior involves both yes and no behaviors. Assertive people often develop a healthy self-confidence that frees them to be even more willing to volunteer for jobs and projects they're particularly qualified for and interested in doing.

An interesting bonus is that the time to do the job and the confidence to volunteer often come from a person's ability to say no to requests that don't match his or her gifts and that would take time away from a project for which that person is particularly suited. The genuinely assertive person can assess requests for time and services and choose whether to say yes or no.

6. Will becoming assertive change me so much I won't even recognize myself?

One of the most important outcomes as individuals learn to be assertive is that they actually become more authentically themselves. They frequently gain a sense of self that is truly God-pleasing in its honesty and openness. The genuinely assertive person is a person of integrity and wholeness, a person whose words and behaviors are consistent with his or her beliefs and values. The genuinely assertive person accurately reflects on the outside what is on the inside.

God Will Do Great Things

This book about assertiveness is written *by* Christians *for* Christians. As you learn about assertiveness and act on what you learn, God will bless you both spiritually and psychologically. You will then be a greater blessing to the people with whom you live, work, and worship.

Bring to your reading of this book your positive expectations and your faith in God's power to continually transform you into the person God wants you to be. God will do great things!

PART ONE

What Is Assertiveness?

1

Passive, Aggressive, and Assertive

"That may be the biggest Christmas tree I've ever seen!" Hank Mason, head of the Property Maintenance Committee, stood admiring the 20-foot evergreen and allowed himself to bask for a moment in his excitement and satisfaction. "I'm glad we decided to have one big tree instead of two smaller ones," he added.

Tom Warren, one of the committee members who was spending his Saturday morning helping set up the huge tree in the chancel, looked at the tree with some misgivings.

"It sure does look nice," Tom said loudly enough for everyone to hear, then added in a somewhat uncertain tone, "I only hope the tree stand is sturdy enough to hold it."

Tom waited, hoping that Hank would ask him about his concerns. Having been in charge of putting up Christmas trees at his previous congregation for the past six years, Tom knew all about the hazards of large, unstable Christmas trees. From experience, he had already learned that a tree that size needed guy wires to make sure it didn't fall. People could even be injured if such a large, unstable tree fell. But this was Tom's first Christmas at the new church, and he didn't want people to think he was some pushy know-it-all. He hoped Hank would pick up on his "hint."

Hank picked up on the hint all right, but not in the way Tom intended. Shrugging off Tom's remark with a look of disdain, Hank exclaimed, "Don't be silly! That tree stand is sturdy enough to hold a tree twice that size."

"We might need guy wires," Tom ventured hesitantly.

"Guy wires!" Hank said with a smirk. "Take it easy. Some people always think something awful is going to happen. Let's just get this tree up. I've got other things to do today."

Tom felt the blood rushing to his face, an obvious confirmation of the anger and embarrassment he felt inside. Tom looked away for a moment, hoping Hank and the others hadn't noticed his discomfort at Hank's remarks. Tom had enough trouble handling put-downs outside of church. Getting hit with one in the middle of the sanctuary, though, somehow made it seem even worse.

At that moment Fred, another helper, volunteered to get the boxes of decorations from the storage shed. "Want to help, Tom?"

"Sure," said Tom, glad for an excuse to leave.

Tom and Fred walked toward the storage building. "Tom, don't feel bad about what Hank said. I don't think he realizes how he sounds."

Tom shrugged it off. "Oh, it's okay. No harm done."

But it wasn't okay, and deep inside Tom felt a twinge of guilt. He'd just told Fred a lie to cover up how he felt.

Passive Behavior

Although Tom Warren sometimes behaves assertively or even aggressively, his preferred style of dealing with people is passive. The word *passive* means "not resisting" or "not acting." Originally, the word *passive* was derived from a Latin word meaning "to suffer," which is an accurate description of what often results from passive behavior.

Passive behavior is behavior that moves against the self. Passive behavior says, "I'll give up anything to avoid displeasure and to gain approval." Passive people frequently give up important parts of their own personalities to avoid disapproval or criticism so others will like them.

Certainly Tom Warren suffered that Saturday morning as he helped put up the Christmas tree. Tom's behavior was behavior that moved against himself, because he had knowledge and experience he wanted to offer, yet he behaved passively. He merely hinted at what he knew by his vague comment: "I only hope the tree stand is sturdy enough to hold it." Afraid people would think he was a pushy know-it-all, he resorted to hinting, even when the safety of the congregation was at stake. This bothered Tom's conscience.

Tom also suffered in the face of Hank's "Don't be silly" put-down. By not standing up for himself, Tom suffered the injustice and humiliation of Hank's attack.

His body told him that all was not well by increasing the blood flow to his face. His face turned red, and he felt physically uncomfortable.

Tom again behaved passively when he left the church to help Fred. Tom left Hank to supervise, relinquishing his opportunity to share his knowledge and contribute to the overall safety and success of the project.

Tom moved against himself once more when he told Fred, "It's okay. No harm done." That wasn't true, and Tom again damaged his integrity and compromised his sincerity by not being honest about how he felt. Tom suffered because he moved against himself as he tried to manage public opinion about himself and to hide his feelings.

Passivity may show itself physically or verbally. Tom's passivity was both.

Physical Passivity

Physical passivity is marked by a person's withdrawal from a situation. An individual may walk out, leave the room, sleep too much, or withdraw by using alcohol or other drugs. Another way to be physically passive is to receive physical abuse without defense or protest.

Verbal Passivity

A verbally passive person "keeps quiet." If you're passive in your communications, you withhold feedback.

Consider for a moment the importance of feedback. It

would be very difficult, for example, to function without feedback from your environment. When you walk, certain muscles in your legs send information to the brain about the effects of your leg movements. Because you have feedback from different muscles about how far your leg has moved and where your leg is presently, you can take another step. Your muscles have communicated with your brain, and your brain has communicated with your muscles. Without this exchange of communication, you couldn't walk. You would collapse.

In the same way, when you withhold feedback in a personal relationship, you risk the collapse of that relationship. If you withhold needed information when you communicate, you create an atmosphere of uncertainty. The other person never really knows what you think or feel. He or she is left to assume what you're thinking and feeling, and assumptions can lead to disastrous misunderstandings and strained relationships.

Verbal passivity also involves such behaviors as pretending to remember someone's name, lying, hinting, pretending to understand, or falsely saying, "That's okay." Christians are often tempted to say "I forgive you" prematurely, just to avoid the painful process of acknowledging and working through a sin and its consequences. It may take a long, painful time for the other to come to genuine repentance.

Living in a predominately passive style is much like living out a lifelong game of "Mother, May I?" In "Mother, May I?" you can't make a move without the permission of the person who is "Mother." Similarly, when people adopt a passive style, they're constantly alert to the potential displeasure and disapproval of others and will fine-tune their lives and activities in order to gain the permission and approval of those they deem powerful.

Aggressive Behavior

Aggressive behavior is behavior that moves against others. Aggressive behavior says, "I have the right to patronize you, put you down, dominate you, or humiliate you in order to get what I want." The aggressive person has few internal restraints and recognizes few external limits.

Hank Mason behaved aggressively in his dealings with Tom. Specifically, his behavior moved against Tom when he said, "Don't be silly," dismissing Tom's concern. Granted, it isn't Hank's responsibility to chase down every hint Tom throws into the conversational arena, but some sensitivity to Tom's misgivings and a well-placed question or two might have shifted the focus from Hank's need to be in charge to a discussion of Tom's experience and suggestions.

Hank's behavior also moved against others because his refusal to entertain Tom's misgivings actually put the congregation in danger. Having never erected a 20-foot tree before, Hank wasn't aware of what he didn't know. Neither was he receptive to the doubts of others. By moving against Tom, Hank also moved against the safety and best interest of the congregation.

Aggression may be physical, nonverbal, or verbal, or it may surface as *passive aggression.*

Physical Aggression

You are all too familiar with physical acts of aggression from reading daily news reports of abused spouses, children, and older people. You hear of murders, assaults, drive-by shootings, and gang warfare. You doubtless know more than you want to know about physical aggression.

Nonverbal Aggression

Nonverbal aggression is familiar to anyone who knows the phrase "If looks could kill." Many aggressive communications take place without words. Individuals move against others simply by facial expression, by their gestures, or by their tone of voice. Consider how someone feels attacked when he or she says something and another responds with a sneer or a look of scorn. Hank's smirk was an instance of nonverbal aggression. Sometimes people shake their heads in disbelief or utter a disgusted snort, a barely audible "humph," or an exasperated, exaggerated sigh to show that they think what a person has just said is so stupid that it's not worth considering. People use these aggressive behaviors to move against others, trying to establish superiority over them.

Verbal Aggression

Most aggressive acts are verbal rather than physical, and many social situations are war zones where words are weapons. Verbal aggression takes several forms:

• *Insults.* The word *insult* comes from a Latin word meaning "to leap upon." Some people verbally "leap upon" others, with words or by the tone of their voices. Sometimes people use taunts that are hurtful not because of the actual meaning of the words, but because the intended meaning is the opposite of the spoken meaning: "Of course it is," they say in a condescending, sarcastic tone, implying, "Of course it isn't, you dummy."

• *Put-downs.* The term *put-down* is a fitting description of verbal aggression. People use put-downs to place another in an inferior position by calling attention to faults or mistakes or by telling others something unflattering about the person while the person is present. A put-down is used to humiliate or demean another person.

• *Profanity.* Profanity often accompanies put-downs and other aggressive behaviors. Most people have become accustomed to hearing profanity and seldom think about what it means and how it affects interpersonal relations. Profanity almost automatically transforms what is said into aggressive communication. Consider the difference between these two statements made by a tired father to his son:

"Would you please move your arm out of the way. I

can't see the football game," *or* "Damn it, get your arm out of the way. I can't see."

The usual excuse is that profanity supplies emphasis or forcefulness, and that's true. People often use profanity when they want to forcefully make their point, to help them manipulate or dominate an encounter. It's a "you'd-better-listen-to-this" communication.

• *Blaming.* The word *blame* originates in an old French word meaning "to speak evil of," and that's essentially what someone does when he or she places blame on another. Frequently, the root of blame is applying one's own personal "shoulds" or "oughts" to others. Others should do thus-and-so. Others ought to think so-and-so. And if they don't let me live their lives for them, then what happens is their fault. Blame usually escalates aggression. Certainly instances arise in which one person is truly to blame for a problem, but in most conflicts both people have contributed to the problem.

• *Sarcasm.* The word *sarcasm* in its Greek roots means "flesh tearing." Anyone who has felt the pain of a sarcastic remark will appreciate that apt description. Sarcasm tears psychological flesh. Sarcasm is always aggressive, and it almost always hurts much more than the physical pain of a slap or a cut. Sarcastic comments from your childhood made by a teacher, a parent, or a classmate may still hurt when you recall them today.

With all these ways to be verbally aggressive, it's no wonder that James wrote to the early Christians:

> How great a forest is set ablaze by a small fire! And the tongue is a fire. The tongue is placed among our members as a world of iniquity; it stains the whole body, sets on fire the cycle of nature, and is itself set on fire by hell. For every species of beast and bird, of reptile and sea creature, can be tamed and has been tamed by the human species, but no one can tame the tongue—a restless evil, full of deadly poison. With it we bless the Lord and Father, and with it we

curse those who are made in the likeness of God.
From the same mouth come blessing and cursing.
My brothers and sisters, this ought not to be so
(James 3:5b–10 NRSV).

Passive Aggression

Passive aggression is a subtle kind of aggression, an underhanded way of moving against another person or manipulating others to get one's own way. Those who use passive aggression are sometimes called "powerful passives" because they use undercover means to get their way, to get even, and to express what they're not willing to say in a straightforward manner.

Passive aggression may take several forms:

• *Procrastinating, forgetting, dawdling.* This kind of passive aggression looks a lot like a sit-down strike because in both instances people are attempting to get their way by inactivity. Despite promises and assurances that they'll do their best, they hold back and actually sabotage the goals and plans of others.

• *Pouting.* People who pout are like a bean pot—you know something is cooking because you can see the steam escape! Usually people who pout deny that anything is bothering them. If you ask what's wrong, they answer, "Nothing."

• *Silent treatment.* Here's a new twist to an old saying:

Sticks and stones are hard on bones,
Aimed with an angry art.
Words can sting like anything,
But silence breaks the heart.

A person who uses the silent treatment is trying to punish the other, trying to inflict pain. This passive-aggressive behavior is often successful because to be shunned and ignored is to have your existence denied; the silent treatment is a way of saying, "You're not even here." Such withholding of love and relationship is painful indeed.

• *Manipulative tears.* Those who use tears manipulatively generate them for the express purpose of getting their own way. Manipulative tears are not to be confused with heartfelt tears or tears shed in spite of one's attempt to keep from crying.

Assertive Behavior

Assertive behavior is integral and essential to the Christian lifestyle. Assertive behavior is behavior that honors the self while honoring others. The assertive person authentically cares for others and at the same time engages in God-pleasing self-care.

Assertive behavior is a constructive way of living and relating to other people. It reflects your concern about being honest, direct, open, and natural in your relations with others.

Assertiveness encompasses a wide variety of actions. For example, assertive behavior may involve standing up for your rights. It may involve genuinely expressing your affection for another person. Assertive behavior may mean giving as well as receiving compliments. And it might involve saying yes to some requests and no to other requests.

By behaving assertively, people begin to see themselves and others as individuals who are important and who have feelings, ideas, opinions, and rights that are worthy of expression. Assertive behavior can mean expressing all those aspects of self without resorting to threats, hostility, manipulation, or other aggressive actions. And it can mean experiencing those expressions from others without considering oneself threatened, abused, intimidated, or victimized.

Expressions of assertiveness are as individual as each person. Only Jesus could be 100 percent assertive 100 percent of the time (though at times he chose not to be). For the rest of humanity, some people are more assertive and some people are less so. Most people are more comfortable being assertive in some situations than in others. For example, one person may be very assertive in standing up for her rights before a manipulative door-to-door salesperson, but she may be reluctant to be assertive with a manipulative coworker.

This kind of personal unevenness characterizes the normal learning process, so it's no surprise that it's also true of learning assertion skills. Even though you may understand assertiveness very well and use assertive language and behaviors regularly and enthusiastically, you may still absolutely shock yourself from time to time by responding aggressively or passively out of habit.

When—not if—this happens, be kind to yourself. Give yourself a pat on the back for being able to identify a nonassertive response, and take just a moment to think about what you'll do next time. And then let it go. Inconsistency is a legitimate part of the normal learning curve. You can't develop new patterns without occasionally slipping back into old ones. Concentrate on what you've done well.

Assertive Attitudes and Behaviors

These attitudes and behaviors characterize Christians who live assertively.

• *Assertive Christians believe they have options.* They believe that, because God has given them a free will, they are to exercise that will and critically examine options and opportunities so they can make God-pleasing decisions.

• *Assertive Christians are proactive.* The word *proactive* means "to move forward" or "to move ahead of events." An assertive individual is proactive rather than reactive. He or she will enter into situations and propose ideas, offer opinions, or anticipate needs so as to contribute fully rather than simply react to people or events.

• *Assertive Christians believe God values each person.* "For God so loved the world . . ." affirms the assertive Christian. Scripture repeatedly reveals a God whose care is personal, sacrificial, and focused on each individual.

• *Assertive Christians are motivated by love.* Having experienced God's love and saving grace in Jesus, assertive Christians want to live out that love in all their relationships, including their relationship with themselves.

• *Assertive Christians stand up for themselves without excessive anxiety.* Because their personal value and intrinsic worth depend not on the approval of others but on God's unconditional love and approval, assertive Christians ask others for respect, fair treatment, and honest interactions without excessive anxiety and fearfulness. Assertive Christians participate courageously in personal relationships.

• *Assertive Christians are people of integrity.* The word integrity means "wholeness," and assertive individuals are people who strive to live out their faith, to integrate what they believe and how they live. For an assertive Christian, the outside reveals the inside.

• *Assertive Christians accept their own limitations and the limitations of others.* There is no perfect world, and Jesus was the only perfect person. We have limits to our time, energy, and abilities. Assertive Christians can live with their limitations and understand that others also have limitations.

• *Assertive Christians practice self-revelation within appropriate personal boundaries.* Assertive people make decisions about what personal information they want to share with others and what they would prefer to keep to themselves. Assertive individuals then uphold those personal decisions.

• *Assertive Christians can choose to behave assertively, aggressively, or passively.* In chapter 4, you'll examine Jesus' life and the choices he made. At appropriate times Jesus chose to behave occasionally passively, sometimes aggressively, most often assertively.

• *Assertive Christians believe that every person has certain basic human rights.* Even though some mistakenly malign personal rights as self-serving and sinful, the assertive Christian discovers human rights throughout Scripture and in Jesus' life. Assertive individuals honor human rights for others and claim them for themselves as well. See appendix B for a partial listing of basic human rights.

St. Paul Writes to Timid Timothy

Individuals who think and behave assertively are people who have an active orientation to life, people who participate fully in life, people with a sense of God-given personal power. Assertive men and women live decisively, aware that life is full of choices and sensitive to their responsibility to make decisions about those choices.

While assertive Christians may not always know immediately which decision they want to make, they move deliberately toward information and people, ask for the time necessary to make a good decision, and feel free to modify or change that decision, should that change be appropriate.

Paul wrote to the young pastor Timothy: "The Spirit that God has given us does not make us timid; instead, his Spirit fills us with power, love, and self-control" (2 Timothy 1:7 TEV).

Paul is telling Timothy that the Holy Spirit's presence gives Christians courage in their personal relationships. As the Holy Spirit fills us with power, we all have a growing ability to make careful choices based on our faith and on our personal understanding of God's will for our lives. As the Holy Spirit fills us with God's love, we thank God that we can by God's power behave selflessly, respectfully, and compassionately toward others. And, as the Holy Spirit fills us with self-control, we accept responsibility for our behavior, live a life accountable to God, and approach challenges and life tasks with perseverance.

With God's Spirit alive in us, we can rise above timidity and be faithful and strong in the Lord. With God's Spirit alive in us, we can be assertive!

2

The Assertive Lifestyle

The conditions for sailing had unexpectedly become dangerous for participants in the 1988 Olympic sailing competition outside Seoul, Korea. Acceptable winds of 15 knots had escalated at times to as much as 35 knots, and the waves were playing havoc with boats and crews. During the fifth of seven races, two sailors of the Singapore team were thrown into the water, suffering injuries. They struggled unsuccessfully to right their boat.

Lawrence Lemieux of Edmonton, Canada, was sailing alone near the halfway point in that race, exhilarated by the challenge of the competition and excited that he held second place in the race and was likely to win a medal.

When Lemieux saw the Singapore boat capsize, flinging its two sailors into the choppy sea, he immediately abandoned his race and headed toward the sailors. While dragging the first sailor into the boat, Lemieux saw that his boat was beginning to fill with water. Nevertheless, Lemieux headed toward the second sailor, who was clinging to his overturned boat. Rescuing him also, Lemieux waited for a patrol boat to transfer the two men.

The time he lost in making the rescue put Lemieux out of competition, and he finished 21st of 33 starters.

Lawrence Lemieux was a true Olympian, a man who won a different kind of medal that day—an intangible medal bestowed by an astonished and admiring world, a medal of honor for his character, compassion, and integrity. By deeming the rescue more important than the Olympic medal, Lemieux revealed the exemplary character of an Olympic winner and reminded the world that Olympic greatness is as much a matter of who you are as what you do.

In much the same way, assertiveness is not only something you do. Assertiveness is a way you are. Assertiveness grows out of your maturity and your ability to know and respect yourself as an individual, an individual unique by God's design. Assertiveness is one of the outward signs of an integrated personality.

Just as Christians participate in a lifelong struggle to live a life fully obedient to God, so the development of an integrated personality is a lifelong process of personal growth. An integrated personality has all its separate parts joined and blended, the end result being personal wholeness and completeness. A well-integrated personality is a unified personality.

Of course, the fully integrated personality is the ideal. Human beings are all less than fully integrated. In fact, one of the life tasks for everyone is to move in the direction of more fully integrating all the separate components of his or her personality.

Some of the individual parts that people strive to bring together into a unified whole are personal manner, attitudes, faith life, choice of possessions, personal value system, orientation toward others, feelings, behaviors, thinking patterns, and learning. This chapter takes a closer look at several of those components: faith life, thinking and feeling, and behavioral choices.

Assertiveness Is about Living Your Faith

Contemplating the process of integration is especially exciting and hopeful for Christians because God deeply desires that his people be whole, complete, and fully integrated. And God is willing to put himself and his resources into the process. God is willing to supply, through the power of the Holy Spirit, the wholeness you need. What was whole at creation was broken and fragmented by sin, and Jesus has come personally into history and into individual lives to restore wholeness—partially restored now, fully restored when he comes again. That is why you can so confidently engage God's power and trust God's Spirit in your quest for wholeness and in your work toward a more integrated personality.

Two characteristics of the life of faith that help personal integration are consistency and authenticity.

Consistency

Assertive Christians want to live a life that is in agreement with their faith, with their calling to be God's people. Assertive Christians strive to make choices and decisions that will be consistent with their knowledge of God's will and in harmony with their experience of God's faithfulness. And assertive Christians take seriously St. Paul's admonition to "live a life worthy of the calling you have received" (Ephesians 4:1 NIV).

God's power is the most important factor in unifying a Christian's life and personality. God's power pulls Christians together and makes them whole. As you cooperate with God, you experience and live out the wholeness God wants in your life. And remember, when you fail to be consistent and your life doesn't match your faith, God's forgiveness is there for you.

Authenticity

The Christian faith life is real in the fullest sense of the word. You can be free of many of the debilitating fears, defenses, and pretensions that seem so plausible, so tempting, and so necessary as you make your way through life.

Christians struggle to live lives that are honest and sincere, though, of course, not without sin and its consequences. There is something authentic, honest, and real about Christians who live out their Christian calling in a nondefensive and straightforward manner, who can admit they need a Savior.

Assertiveness Is about Thinking and Feeling

A box of tissues is a familiar sight. If someone held up such a box and asked you what your feelings are about tissues, you might say, "Feelings! What feelings? I don't have any feelings about tissues!"

If you were pressed, however, perhaps thinking about that box would summon up some memories—memories with feelings attached.

A hay fever sufferer, recalling how miserable he'd felt as he sniffled and sneezed his way through the last allergy season, might see that box of tissues with apprehension. The mother of a bride might recall bittersweet memories of joy and sadness at the recent wedding. A widower might remember grief and tears unending.

That box of tissues could have three people recalling three different feelings associated with memories. Where did these feelings come from? Did a box of tissues make them feel apprehensive, bittersweet, or grieved?

Of course not. The brain stores feelings along with sensations and thoughts—and can summon them when prodded, given the right associations. This summoning of memories is very complex and very rapid. Most of the time you're not even aware it's going on. Sometimes, too, your thinking process is closed to you because the thoughts are on an unconscious level, though the feelings may rise to the surface.

Thoughts Sometimes Come First, Then Feelings

One way to explain how feelings surface is to say that feelings can follow thoughts. Feelings can be a reflection and indication of your thoughts.

Many people find this concept difficult to accept because of its implications. If indeed some feelings arise from your thoughts, then some of the emotions you experience are the consequence of your thoughts. Believing this, a person would find it hard to say with integrity, "You make me so angry!" A more accurate statement would be, "I make me so angry!" And most accurate of all would be, "I'm angry!"

The fact is, no one can make you mad. No one can make you feel a certain way, even though another individual can provide the circumstances in which you're more likely to choose a particular feeling. But in the end, others don't have control over you and your feelings. You do.

Thoughts Can Modify Feelings

Knowing you can control your feelings means knowing you can choose to create your own emotions to a great extent by what you choose to think about people and events.

Individuals are response-able: This concept is one of the fundamental principles upon which this book is based. The assertive Christian is able to respond in various ways to people and events. The assertive Christian makes choices.

Human beings are complex creatures. Sometimes people choose anger as the appropriate response to a certain behavior while at other times they passively accept that same behavior. Sometimes when a two-year-old has a tantrum, a parent feels anxious and embarrassed; at other times that same parent may ignore the behavior with hardly a second thought. One day you might feel hurt when a friend doesn't call; on another day you might feel relieved that the friend forgot to call because now you can finish that novel. The assertive person can consider many possible responses and then choose the most helpful and appropriate response. Assertive people refuse to be helpless, hopeless victims who have no choices or options.

However, others can create situations in which, for example, it's easier to choose anger than to choose an alternative response. Everyone experiences some situations in which he or she habitually chooses anger. Now, in some situations it's very appropriate to choose anger or sadness. But human beings are not reactive robots who have no control over what they do. They are thinking, feeling, processing creatures who are capable of exercising control over their own behavior. And that gives hope, because it means you can change the way you react in certain situations if you're unhappy with the way you behave.

If you tie your emotional well-being to other people's behavior, you'll probably be upset a great deal of the time. Rarely will people dedicate their lives to behaving only in ways that are designed to make you happy. You must own your feelings, and you must accept responsibility for modifying your feelings. If you can accept the fact that other people are not directly causing your emotional life, you can then give attention to your own thinking. Thinking is the process by which you sometimes generate your feelings and the process you can also use to change those feelings.

An assertive lifestyle includes thinking that focuses on the truth, identifies and challenges irrational beliefs, and celebrates what God has done.

Assertive Thinking Focuses on the Truth

"Have nothing to do with godless myths," St. Paul tells Timothy (1 Timothy 4:7 NIV). Most Christians are occasionally tempted to embrace godless myths when their thinking begins to dwell on anxieties, old angers, or fears about the future. Those are godless preoccupations. When people dwell on those fearful topics, they're tempted to deal with their anxieties in ways that don't invite God into the process.

The truth is that God earnestly desires to be a part of your thinking and problem solving. You can learn to face anxieties, bitterness, and fear because God will inform your thinking and give you wisdom and insight. You don't have to resort to trying to fool yourself with unrealistic positive thinking or by minimizing the challenges you face. You can give up rationalizing and intellectualizing, if those are typical patterns for you. You can learn to face the truth because you are confident of God's presence.

Assertive Thinking Identifies and Challenges Irrational Beliefs

Sometimes people's thinking is so influenced by their emotions that they "can't think straight," and their thinking is neither logical nor truthful. At those times, irrational beliefs may form the basis for their choices and decisions. Sometimes called "stinkin' thinkin'," irrational beliefs usually arouse excessive anxiety in people. A few of those irrational beliefs are:

- If someone is angry with me, it must be my fault.

- If others don't tell me I'm a good person, then I must not be.

- It's my duty to make everyone comfortable and happy.

- It's my duty to please everyone all the time.

- Everybody ought to be nice to me.

- I should always be and act happy in spite of any hardship or trouble that comes my way.

Assertive thinking seeks the truth by challenging irrational beliefs and by trying to determine what is unreasonable, illogical, or absurd, and then rejecting those thoughts.

Assertive Thinking Celebrates What God Has Done

When you think truthfully about the people and events in your life, you'll probably experience less anxiety. You then have the ability to think clearly and to challenge some of your untruthful, irrational beliefs and self-messages.

When you refuse to concentrate exclusively on your anxieties and fears and instead look for the truth, you can celebrate what God has done and continues to do in your life.

You can celebrate the fact that God equips you for the tasks and challenges that confront you. You can celebrate the truth that God is always with you, holding fast to this promise: "I will never leave you nor forsake you" (Joshua 1:5b NIV). You can celebrate God's personal presence and protection, and you can therefore live with fewer defenses, greater peace, and wonderful confidence.

Assertive thinking focuses on the truth, challenges irrational beliefs, and celebrates God's presence. Assertive thinking keeps you in touch with the God of everlasting and unchanging truth.

Assertiveness Is about Behavior Choices

Not only are you able to make choices about your thinking, you can also make choices about your behavior. The most visible evidence that you are behaving in a responseable manner is that you can actually choose behaviors that give evidence of your faith life and that are an outward sign of your assertive thinking.

Assertive Behavior Means Speaking Respectfully about Yourself and Others

"I'm a loser!" "I'll never amount to anything!" "I'm such an idiot!"

"He's a moron!" "She's an airhead!" "What a bozo!"

These expressions are examples of the disrespectful language people sometimes use when talking about themselves or others. Disrespectful and derogatory language and labels often indicate that the speaker is confusing the person with his or her behavior.

For example, someone who commits a thoughtless act is not necessarily a thoughtless person. If you forgot to stop at the grocery store to buy milk on the way home from work, you can make a deliberate choice about how you interpret that act. You could choose to berate yourself, call yourself uncomplimentary names, and make an issue of your presumed lack of personal competence.

A healthier and more useful choice would be to focus on the behavior, not the person, and simply look at the truth of the matter: you forgot to stop at the grocery on your way home. Period. It isn't necessary to attribute motives or assess your overall human competence.

Those who confuse a person with his or her behavior are often overgeneralizing. To overgeneralize is to use one incident (or a few) to make a judgment about that person's overall ability or competence. The truth is, a single negative event is not the same as an endless pattern of poor performance. Assertive thinking focuses on the truth, and assertive behavior acts on the truth.

You learn to deal truthfully and fairly with yourself and others by paying attention to the way God treats you. God doesn't confuse you with your behavior. It is abundantly clear in Scripture that God is a just God who hates sinful behavior. And it is abundantly clear that even though God may at times hate a person's behavior, God dearly, personally, and individually loves each person. God hasn't said, "I'll love you when you're more like me." In fact, Romans 5:8b (TEV) says, "It was while we were still sinners that Christ died for us!"

Assertive Behavior Means Making Choices about Stewardship of Time

You have the freedom to exercise choice in your decisions about how you use time.

You are the expert. You are the only one who knows how much time you need alone, how much time you need with others, and how much time you need for spiritual enrichment and adequate care for your body. You are the only one who can make those and many other decisions about how you use your time. Jesus, for example, frequently chose to go away from the crowd to be alone and to escape the incessant demands of public ministry.

You can also make appropriate choices about how you

apportion your time for God-pleasing self-care and sacrificial care for others. For instance, if you need a full eight hours of sleep but seldom get it, you can make some new choices about how much rest you intend to get. Or if you want to serve others by helping adults learn to read but never seem to have the time to be a tutor, you can make choices and changes so that you have time to serve in that way. Assertive behavior involves assessing your personal needs and deciding to meet those needs in a God-pleasing manner, using the gift of time as one means of meeting those needs.

Assertive Behavior Means Making Choices about Friendships

Individuals can assertively choose to initiate or end a friendship, to establish personal boundaries about how close a friendship may become, or to maintain and celebrate long-standing friendships.

How you participate in a friendship is an assertive personal choice. You may choose, for example, to initiate a friendship with another person, understanding that the other individual may or may not respond positively to your gesture of friendship. The other person also has the right of personal choice and is free to refuse the offered friendship.

In the same manner, you can assertively make choices about the depth and intimacy of your relationships. Assertive behavior expresses personal preference in matters of interpersonal closeness.

Assertive behaviors help you maintain and enhance existing friendships. When you initiate phone calls, suggest plans for time together, or express affection and appreciation, you behave in a proactive, assertive manner that affirms the value of your relationships and enhances their development.

Assertive Behavior Means Making Choices about Christian Servanthood

God gives each Christian marvelous opportunities for ministry. In fact, Christians are generally aware of more needs and more opportunities than any one person could possibly meet in a single lifetime. People must make choices.

As you live under the grace of God, you can enthusiastically say yes to those ministries to which you believe God is calling you. Always, you recognize that God sometimes calls you to sacrifice as you care for others, to walk an extra mile, to experience pain and suffering as well as joy in Christian service. You do what you can as God directs you, and then you accept the fact that God will call other Christians to meet the needs you see but cannot meet yourself.

Assertive Christians make deliberate, prayerful choices about where and how they'll serve and accept the fact that they may need to review and revise those commitments from time to time.

An assertive lifestyle invites the merging of your faith life, thinking patterns, and behavior choices. Such a harmonious blending of these distinct parts of your life and personality leads you toward a wholeness that pleases God.

3

What Is Assertiveness For?

Merv Griffin, former television talk show host, jet-setter, darling of the rich and famous, and entrepreneur, found himself holding a microphone once again as he hosted an international bodybuilders' event at his Las Vegas hotel. On stage were half a dozen champion bodybuilders, posing and posturing, first flexing one muscle group and then contracting another.

The audience was a standing-room-only crowd of bodybuilder fans who hooted, whistled, applauded, and generally voiced appreciation for the champions' spectacular muscular development, the reward for an immense investment of time, energy, and dedication.

After some introductory remarks, Griffin confessed that he had a burning curiosity about just one thing. And so, moving admiringly from champion to champion, Griffin held the microphone in front of each person and asked, "Can you tell me, just what are muscles for?"

The first person looked startled, then changed position without answering. The second glared annoyance at his questioner and turned to display a spectacular group of back muscles to the enthusiastic crowd. A puzzled Griffin moved among the champions, asking each the same question: "What are muscles for?" Griffin never got an answer.

Before plunging single-mindedly and enthusiastically into developing your assertiveness "muscles," you need to be able to clearly answer the question, what is assertiveness for?

Consider this: Assertiveness helps you get along better with others, with yourself, and with God. When you think and behave assertively, you can expect positive results in a number of areas.

Assertiveness Helps You Get Along with Others

Because assertive behavior is behavior that respects others, increasing your assertiveness knowledge and skills will improve your personal relationships. Assertive individuals work for authentic personal relations, recognize the power of mutual respect, understand that their behavior influences the behavior choices of others, and know that they are contributing to the well-being of the whole community.

Assertive Individuals Work for Authentic Personal Relations

An authentic personal relationship is a relationship in which each person relates to the other with honesty and genuineness. Assertiveness usually improves communication because assertiveness means being honest, direct, and open in a natural way when relating to others.

Many of the communication behaviors that damage relationships with others are nonassertive—that is, either passive or aggressive. Those communication styles aren't helpful because they allow people either to hide their thoughts and feelings (passive) or invite increased defensiveness on the part of the other (aggressive). Assertive communication skills help people reveal true opinions, real feelings, honest differences, and precious hopes and dreams.

Assertive communication helps individuals get to know each other because they are able to give up manipulative games, half-truths, insincere smiles, and attempts to control and possess others.

Because assertiveness requires you to give up controlling behaviors that may have provided a sense of safety and security, assertive communication invites you to risk as you relate. Your growing assertiveness allows a new sense of inner security—you know you can prayerfully, deliberately, and carefully consider options, make decisions, and behave respectfully toward yourself and others without ever resorting to games or manipulation.

Aggressive, Passive, and Assertive Behavior Can Influence the Behavior of Others

Human beings are curious creatures. Perfectly free to choose their own behaviors, they still often look at the behavior of others for cues as to how they should act. Aggressive, passive, and assertive behaviors each invite others to respond in particular ways.

• *Aggressive Behavior.* Aggressive behavior creates a situation in which others tend to respond either passively or aggressively. Many people describe their reactions to aggressive people who shout, threaten, or insult them by saying, "I just walked away," or "I was so overwhelmed I couldn't think of a thing to say." Such aggressive behavior, which can bring out the passivity in others, looks like this:

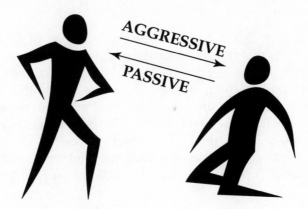

At other times, aggressive behavior can lead others to respond aggressively in return. Aggressive responses might include shouting back, revenge, physical attack, or matching insult for insult. Such an aggressive exchange might look like this:

• *Passive Behavior.* A serious consequence of behaving passively is that it can encourage others to behave passively. For example, the last time Bill sat in a church council meeting, he said nothing during the entire meeting. He had thoughts, feelings, and reactions to the issue being discussed, yet he chose to say nothing. Perhaps others made the same choice. As a result, the meeting was not only minimally productive, it was also dull and lifeless: It seemed to last forever. A passive-passive interaction looks like this:

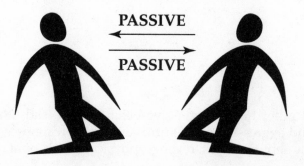

Behaving passively can also be an invitation for others to act aggressively. People who don't stand up for their rights are prime targets for being pushed around and abused by others who have little respect for them. Behaving passively helps neither you nor others. Such a relationship might look like this:

• *Assertive Behavior.* Compare the meeting in which you chose passive behaviors to another meeting where you felt energized, enthused, committed, and involved. No doubt your full and assertive participation in that meeting encouraged others to take part, discuss, volunteer, or simply to care about what was going on. An assertive-assertive exchange would look like this:

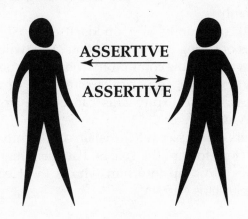

When you directly and honestly express your own thoughts, feelings, and preferences, you encourage others to do so. As you assume your own fair share of the responsibility for decision making and contribute to the success of the meeting, you encourage others to participate and accept their fair share of responsibility as well. Assertive behavior can bring out the best and most mature reactions in people.

Assertive Individuals Contribute to the Well-Being of the Whole Community

Becoming assertive in your relationships goes a long way to enhance the well-being of the whole community. St. Paul speaks of the result of honest, caring interactions:

> Speaking the truth in love, we will in all things grow up into him who is the Head, that is, Christ. From him the whole body, joined and held together by every supporting ligament, grows and builds itself up in love, as each part does its work (Ephesians 4:15–16 NIV).

Paul says that a community will function properly if all the individual parts fit together and work together. A properly functioning community needs the consistent, assertive contributions of its people and their sharing of ideas, feelings, and faith.

Such a community also builds itself up by frequent expressions of caring and appreciation. And, when tensions and conflict arise in the community, the whole community is blessed by assertive, respectful expressions of anger and unhappiness. Those expressions can be the first steps in negotiation for change.

Members of an assertive Christian community are taking important steps toward the goal St. Paul held high: "We will in all things grow up into him who is the Head, that is, Christ" (Ephesians 4:15 NIV).

Assertiveness Helps You Get Along with Yourself

Do you confidently share your opinions and beliefs with others? Do you become angry when people take advantage of you, either boiling on the inside while saying nothing (passive) or losing control of your temper (aggressive)? Do you frequently fail to ask for things you really want? Have you ever felt guilty and angry with yourself because you couldn't say no to a request? Are you indecisive? Do you ever want to compliment someone but feel too embarrassed? Or, for that matter, do you become embarrassed when people compliment you?

People who don't assert themselves, who typically behave either passively or aggressively, usually feel anger toward themselves and others, a sense of being taken for granted and unappreciated; they may even experience headaches and other physical complaints. Sometimes people who don't assert themselves experience a sense of loss or remorse for the compliment they didn't give or the affectionate word they failed to share.

But practicing assertive behavior frequently increases self-esteem and self-confidence, helps you take care of your body by lowering anxiety levels, and helps you deal with uncomfortable emotions such as anger or guilt. Assertiveness also helps with your efforts at problem solving.

Assertive Behavior Works to Increase Self-Esteem and Self-Confidence

Former Dallas Cowboys head coach Tom Landry was lecturing his players after a game in which they had repeatedly danced, wiggled, and spiked the ball in the end zone after each touchdown. In spite of rules to the contrary, his young players insisted on celebrating every time they scored. "Act like you've been in the end zone before," he admonished.

Coach Landry wanted his players to be seen as mature, competent, confident, professional football players, not inexperienced rookies who couldn't quite believe they had actually scored a touchdown!

In much the same way, as you learn to be more consistently assertive in situations where you've behaved aggressively or passively in the past, you will begin to see yourself as a competent, confident person. And it doesn't take long for that enhanced confidence and increased self-esteem to show on the outside.

Assertiveness Contributes to Physical Well-Being

Medical researchers have found that the emotional state most likely to lead to heart disease isn't constant worry, stress, or even chronic hurrying. The emotional state most damaging to physical health is chronic anger.

People who are chronically angry are in a constant state of physical excitation, the same kind of excitation you would experience if you were suddenly to see a tiger while you were walking in the jungle, a kind of physical Red Alert. God designed your body so that the rare alarm would give you the enormous burst of energy, adrenaline, and glucose you need to fight or flee. If, however, your everyday life is so filled with unresolved anger and its accompanying stress that you live in a rather constant state of Red Alert, your body might pay the price with stress-related illness.

Assertive individuals are more likely to deal with anger at the time it occurs, whether it's their own anger or another person's anger. They have learned not to be intimidated or manipulated by another's attempts to make them feel scared, guilty, or anxious.

Your physical well-being is also improved when you learn to say an assertive no to those things that may injure your health. If you've decided to say no to excessive alcohol, drugs, cigarettes, or fatty foods, assertion skills will serve you well when well-meaning friends or family members try to change your mind or tempt you with "Just one!"

Assertive Behavior Helps with Solving Problems

People are much more effective problem solvers when they approach problems nondefensively. If they feel personally threatened and personally anxious about the problems they encounter, they focus their attention on themselves instead of the problem.

Assertion skills help you get your defensive self out of the way so that your clear-thinking, problem-solving self can listen well, express both thoughts and feelings, consider options, and work to negotiate a mutually satisfying solution to the problem.

Even the best solutions to problems may require review and modification, however, and assertive individuals can participate in such a review without undue anxiety.

While passive and aggressive efforts at problem solving tend to focus on people, assertive efforts focus on the problem and the process of understanding its cause as well as its impact and meaning for the people involved.

Passive problem-solving behaviors such as procrastination, escape, passive-aggressive sneak attacks, or denial of the problem usually only make a problem worse because such behaviors don't work to solve the problem; they may only temporarily relieve the anxiety of the people involved.

Aggressive problem-solving behaviors such as name-calling, blaming, insults, labels, or physical aggression usually escalate a conflict. People who focus on the problem and its solutions instead of on the people involved, however, find that assertion skills serve them well and help them feel good about how they respond and participate in difficult situations.

Assertiveness Helps You Get Along with God

An assertive Christian is a person who is open to God's direction and leading. Assertive Christians are concerned first for God's approval and ask God's help to reject unhealthy social pressure. Because assertive Christians seek to deal with others in a straightforward and honest manner, they want to resist temptations to lie or distort the truth. And assertive Christians cooperate with God in the development of self-control.

Assertiveness Frees You to Do God's Will

"Some folks are too polite to be up to any good," says Christian humorist Kin Hubbard.

Whether you call it politeness, fear of disapproval, or old-fashioned peer pressure, you have most likely learned that you feel uncomfortable when people are not pleased with you.

Being assertive can free you from preoccupation with winning the approval of others and help you to be ready to do the good God wants you to do. Because you can shake off the constraints of social pressure and the need for social-approval-at-any-cost, you can reject the irrational belief that you can (and should) please others all the time. Assertive individuals make decisions about what they want to do independent of social pressure.

While social pressure can contribute to aggressive, hostile behavior, undue social pressure usually involves your being pressured into passive behaviors. Having a strong desire to be liked by other people is human, and it's often coupled with an inordinate fear of being disliked.

But social pressure isn't just a modern problem. King Saul admitted that he had disobeyed God's specific instructions to completely destroy the Amalekites and all their possessions. Saul defended himself by saying, "'I was afraid of the people and so I gave in to them'" (1 Samuel 15:24 NIV).

The Apostle John also identifies the problem of social pressure among Jewish leaders who believed in Jesus but kept their faith secret:

Yet at the same time many even among the leaders believed in him. But because of the Pharisees they would not confess their faith for fear they would be put out of the synagogue; for they loved praise from men more than praise from God (John 12:42–43 NIV).

Assertiveness Frees You to Tell the Truth

It's all too easy to be dishonest. "Little white lies" and reshaping the truth by leaving certain things unsaid are familiar temptations for many Christians. Some people are willing to wink at social lying or to allow a mistaken understanding to go uncorrected if it's to their advantage, but lying has never been acceptable to God. Scripture, in both the Old and New Testaments, proclaims God's admonition to be truthful.

Jesus describes himself in John 14:6 (NIV): "'I am the way and the truth and the life.'" Jesus embodies the truth and Jesus is the standard against which everything else can be measured. In John 1:14 (NIV), the apostle describes Jesus in this way: "The Word became flesh and made his dwelling among us. We have seen his glory, the glory of the One and Only, who came from the Father, full of grace and truth."

Clearly, Jesus is the truth become flesh, and being joined to Christ means that you are not just to tell the truth, you are to live a truthful life. In fact, in Ephesians 4:15, the Greek word that is frequently translated *"speaking* the truth" is actually a verb and could be translated "truthing." You are to behave in such a manner that Jesus the Truth is evident in all you do. Speaking the truth then is only one part of living the truth.

There is another side to this "truthing," and it's evident in the remainder of that phrase from Ephesians 4:15: "Speaking the truth *in love."* When you're living assertively, you're not being called to tell the truth at the expense of others.

Perhaps you've heard this saying: Honesty without love is brutality. "Truthing" is not at all the same as saying everything that's on your mind. It would be cruel to destroy someone else's pleasure—in a new hat, for example—by volunteering the opinion that you think it's the ugliest hat you've ever seen. If you're asked (and you may not be, you know), use your creativity. You could say, "Your pleasure in wearing that hat is beautiful to see. I'm glad to see you so happy."

Assertive behavior is built on the principles of truth and honesty. You are to be honest with God, with yourself, and with those with whom you live and work.

Assertiveness Frees You to Cooperate with God in Developing Self-Control

Galatians 5:23 identifies self-control as a fruit of the Spirit, an evidence that the Holy Spirit is living inside a person. Christians pray that God will expand and extend their capacity and willingness to exercise the self-control they already have.

When you learn to act assertively, you're learning to exercise self-control so that you don't overrespond or underrespond to the circumstances and people in your life. You'll seek to control yourself by the power God gives instead of being controlled by your emotions or by what others say or do.

Assertive behavior enriches, stabilizes, and protects relationships with others, with yourself, and with God. That's what assertiveness is for.

PART TWO

Assertiveness
Is Biblical

4

Jesus Lived Assertively

"Gentle Jesus, meek and mild . . ." Those are familiar words to many Christians. Jesus—so loving, so compassionate, so sacrificial—is the very definition of gentleness and humility. In a world gone mad with aggression and violence, Jesus stands out as a most loving and caring person.

Many Christians may think that Jesus' loving, self-sacrificing attitude and lifestyle mark him as a passive individual, pushed around by life, taken advantage of by countless people, and finally killed. Few people realize how genuinely assertive Jesus was.

It's no wonder that students of Scripture feel a bit confused: some of Jesus' actions appear to be aggressive, and other behaviors appear to be passive. How could Jesus be a loving, compassionate Lord and behave any way except passively? How could a loving, compassionate person call church leaders of his time a "brood of vipers" (Matthew 12:34 NIV)? How could a truly gentle person say, "'I did not come to bring peace, but a sword'" (Matthew 10:34 NIV)? How could a genuinely meek person scold his disciples for not staying awake to pray with him in Gethsemane (Luke 22:46)? And how could a person who had the power to heal refuse to visit a sick friend until after he knew the friend had died (John 11:6)? Jesus did all these things.

In a close look at the Gospels, however, you'll marvel at the healthy balance Jesus demonstrated in his choice of behaviors. Jesus lived assertively, but Jesus also deliberately chose at times to behave passively or aggressively. Because he knew when to use each of those behaviors to accomplish his ministry of salvation most effectively, Jesus sometimes assertively chose to behave in passive or aggressive ways.

Just as Jesus appropriately and assertively balanced his

behavioral choices, so Jesus was in perfect balance as both God and man. Jesus lived out his humanity as all people do, and he used exactly the same spiritual resources that all Christians have available to them: Scripture, prayer, and other believers. And Jesus lived out his Godliness by agreeing to be the sacrifice that would count for all people. Jesus alone could die for the sins of many, opening the door sin had closed between God and the people God loves. Jesus' perfect balance as God and man assures that his behavior was deliberate, decisive, and in harmony with God's will. Jesus' assertiveness served God's purpose.

Jesus Was Assertively Compassionate

Jesus was a compassionate person who, time after time, intently focused on the physical as well as spiritual needs of people. But an interesting pattern emerges when you study the many accounts of healing in the Gospels. Jesus paid attention to the whole person, not only healing the physical illness but tending to the person's spiritual needs as well.

If Jesus had been a passive healer, he had only to wave some kind of magic wand and the person would have experienced physical healing. But Jesus knew that the person's most important need was not for physical relief but for personal wholeness. That's why Jesus was not swayed by the Pharisees' objections to his healing on the Sabbath. Jesus knew that the Pharisees had the wrong priorities in their practice of religion: They emphasized rules and regulations that overshadowed a person's saving relationship with God. To demonstrate God's priorities, Jesus assertively chose to heal the man with the paralyzed hand on the Sabbath. People are more important than rules, and the Sabbath was made to serve the needs of people, not to enslave people.

Then Jesus went back to the synagogue, where there was a man who had a paralyzed hand. Some people were there who wanted to accuse Jesus of doing wrong; so they watched him closely to see whether he would cure the man on the Sabbath. Jesus said to the man, "Come up here to the front." Then he asked the people, "What does our Law allow us to do on the Sabbath? To help or to harm? To save a man's life or to destroy it?"

But they did not say a thing.

Jesus was angry as he looked around at them, but at the same time he felt sorry for them, because they were so stubborn and wrong. Then he said to the man, "Stretch out your hand." He stretched it out, and it became well again (Mark 3:1–5 TEV).

Jesus also dealt assertively with those who wanted to be healed, recognizing the need for individuals to believe that their healing comes from God and knowing that to be well and whole, a person must sincerely desire healing. "Do you want to get well?" Jesus asked the man at the pool of Bethesda (John 5:6 NIV). Jesus assertively involved himself in more than the man's obvious need for physical healing as he invited the man to participate in his own healing.

Jesus actively participated in the lives of people who needed him. His compassion was not a passive sadness at their plight, but an assertive, proactive, caring involvement that commanded response and expected results.

Jesus Followed a Higher Law

Every society has its own rules and regulations about what is acceptable and expected of its members. So society in Jesus' day had its rules about social status, business practices, and religious obligations. Jesus, however, obeyed a higher law, the law of love.

That's why he healed on the Sabbath, respected and honored women, opposed the tyranny of misguided and evil church leaders, and honored those of low social status such as tax collectors and prostitutes.

Jesus assertively defined his ministry and could then

evaluate how prevailing societal norms and rules served or hindered that ministry. An important part of Jesus' ministry was to articulate once more God's will concerning those social rules and norms, especially when society and the church had lost touch with God's will.

Jesus Confronted Lovingly

Jesus' obedience to the law of love pressed him toward loving confrontation. Mark 10 relates the story of Jesus' encounter with a rich young man who wanted to know how to obtain eternal life.

When Jesus told him to keep the commandments, the young man assured Jesus that he had kept all the commandments from his youth. Jesus knew, however, that the young man's heart was firmly planted in his riches and that he was in grave spiritual danger if he couldn't give up his self-righteousness and overwhelming self-sufficiency.

So Jesus "looked straight at him with love" (v. 21 TEV). What a piercing, loving look that must have been! And then Jesus did the most lovingly assertive thing he could do: He told the rich young man to "'sell all you have and give the money to the poor . . . and follow me.'" Jesus made a clear, direct, unmistakably appropriate request that could have been the key to the young man's salvation.

In that poignant moment of opportunity, the rich young man had to make a choice. Jesus respected the fact that each person must make his own life choices and accept the consequences of those choices. Jesus wasn't hampered by a need to control others' actions and decisions in order to ensure the outcome of each of his encounters with people.

The rich young man made a choice: "When the man heard this, gloom spread over his face, and he went away sad, because he was very rich" (v. 22).

Jesus assertively and lovingly confronted the Pharisees who brought him the woman caught in adultery. The Pharisees wanted to trap Jesus and said, "'Teacher, . . . this woman was caught in the very act of committing adultery. In our Law Moses commanded that such a woman must be stoned to death. Now, what do you say?'" (John 8:4–5 TEV).

If Jesus' purpose had been to advance his own standing or to avoid their trap, he could have easily outtalked and outsmarted them. But Jesus had a genuine love for these people who had decided to be his enemies. They had lost sight of the saving purpose of religion amidst all their religiosity and formalities. Like the rich young man, the Pharisees were in grave spiritual danger, beset by self-righteousness and tempted by pride. So Jesus did the most lovingly assertive thing he could do: "As they stood there asking him questions, he straightened up and said to them, 'Whichever one of you has committed no sin may throw the first stone at her'" (v. 7).

Imagine for a moment the effect of Jesus' courageous words as he turned once more to write on the ground. No blazing guns, no haranguing denouncement, no name-calling or dramatic grandstanding. Jesus said what he knew would confront them at their point of greatest need. And then he waited for them to make a choice.

Imagine each man, stone in hand, fired up with righteous indignation at the woman's sin, ready to follow the letter of the law and stone her. Imagine the adrenaline in their veins, the anger in their eyes, the tensing of muscles.

And Jesus' quietly assertive challenge pierced their resolve and drained away their blind self-righteousness. Each man had to remember and confront his own breaking of the law. Perhaps they quietly dropped their rocks to the ground as they silently turned and left the temple.

"When they heard this, they all left, one by one, the older ones first" (v. 9).

Possibly the older Pharisees left first because they had more to remember. Perhaps each member of that crowd in the temple had a conscience-stricken walk home that day. Jesus' assertive and respectful confrontation gives insight into his love for his enemies.

Jesus Assertively Resisted Temptation

Consider the three-year-old's explanation for being in the kitchen, atop a chair, eating cookies from the cookie jar: "I just climbed up to smell them, and my tooth got caught."

While you may smile at a child's rationalizations about cookies or give in to your own temptation to snooze an extra fifteen minutes some morning, Jesus shows an excellent example of assertively resisting temptation in much more important areas of life.

Luke 4:1–13 recounts the story of Jesus' forty days of fasting and temptation in the desert just after his baptism and just before he began his public ministry in Galilee. Jesus was tempted repeatedly throughout those forty days, but three specific temptations are recorded in Luke.

Notice that in each case Jesus responded to the temptation as if he had a choice. And because Jesus had a clear sense of his identity as a person who belonged to God, his sense of personal connection to God shaped and empowered his choices in the face of temptation.

The interaction between Jesus and the devil recorded in Luke 4 is a study in decision making. Clearly, Jesus was free to choose what the devil was offering or it would not have been a real temptation. Indeed, the writer to the Hebrews refers to Jesus' victory over temptation: "For we do not have a high priest who is unable to sympathize with our weaknesses, but we have one who has been tempted in every way, just as we are—yet was without sin" (Hebrews 4:15 NIV).

The devil offered Jesus a choice in each temptation: Order the stone to turn to bread, worship the devil, throw yourself down from the Temple's highest point. And Jesus dealt with each temptation by asserting his personal identity. At his baptism, a voice had come from heaven declaring, "'You are my own dear Son. I am pleased with you'" (Luke 3:22 TEV). Jesus claimed his identity and strength as the Son of God and used it to resist temptation.

By affirming his identity as one who belongs to God and by using the power of Scripture to make clear, direct statements of choice, Jesus resisted temptation assertively.

Jesus Was Not Unduly Influenced by Others

Jesus knew who he was and he knew his mission. While he was consistently involved with others and attentive to them, he was able to be a separate, distinctive "I" in those relationships. His personal integrity, his wholeness, had apparently become a trademark of his unique ministry; even his enemies acknowledged it.

Some Pharisees and some members of Herod's party were sent to Jesus to trap him with questions. They came to him and said, "Teacher, we know that you tell the truth, without worrying about what people think. You pay no attention to a man's status, but teach the truth about God's will for man" (Mark 12:13–14 TEV).

While the Pharisees may have intended to throw Jesus off guard with flattering statements, they spoke the truth.

On another occasion, Jesus' brothers wanted him to go to Jerusalem to celebrate the Festival of Tabernacles. Jesus' brothers were unbelievers, and they urged him to go into the province of Judea even though they (and Jesus) knew that the Jewish authorities were waiting to kill him there.

Jesus didn't respond to his brothers' request with accusations and aggressive attacks upon their character. Instead, his simple assertive reply was:

"The right time for me has not yet come. . . . You go on to the festival. I am not going to this festival, because the right time has not come for me." He said this and then stayed on in Galilee (John 7:6, 8–9 TEV).

Jesus made a choice, announced it in the midst of opposition, and quietly abided by his own decision.

Because Jesus was fully committed to his ministry of salvation, he resisted the influence of well-meaning others who would have distracted him or diverted him from his purpose. Jesus decisively rebukes Peter in Mark 8:31–33 (NRSV):

> Then he began to teach them that the Son of Man must undergo great suffering, and be rejected by the elders, the chief priests, and the scribes, and be killed, and after three days rise again. He said all this quite openly. And Peter took him aside and began to rebuke him. But turning and looking at his disciples, he rebuked Peter and said, "Get behind me, Satan! For you are setting your mind not on divine things but on human things."

At a later time, people brought their children to receive Jesus' blessing, but the disciples scolded them and tried to keep them away. Mark's account shows both Jesus' warm and tender feelings and intentions toward the children and their parents and his anger toward his disciples for their well-meant but inappropriate interference. Jesus intended to bless the children and affirm their parents' faith, and he assertively did so:

> Some people brought children to Jesus for him to place his hands on them, but the disciples scolded the people. When Jesus noticed this, he was angry and said to his disciples, "Let the children come to me, and do not stop them, because the Kingdom of God belongs to such as these. I assure you that whoever does not receive the Kingdom of God like a child will never enter it." Then he took the children in his arms, placed his hands on each of them, and blessed them (Mark 10:13–16 TEV).

Jesus at Times Chose Aggressive or Passive Behavior

Jesus was a model of assertive behavior. Because he focused clearly on his purpose of bringing salvation to all, he gave his attention decisively and compassionately to those he wanted to save. As you examine Jesus' life, you realize his single-mindedness: He knew the purpose of his life (and death), and his every action served that purpose.

Sometimes Jesus chose to behave aggressively in order to fully realize his ministry of salvation. Jesus at times chose aggressive words and behaviors, often directing them against the Pharisees and other religious leaders.

Jesus knew well that the church of his day had become corrupt. Its leaders weren't above bribing witnesses, plotting murders, or collecting exorbitant profits on the sale of animals for sacrifice. The church wasn't centered on God's plan for salvation, nor did it celebrate or honor God's faithful covenant with his people. Church leaders were actually leading the people away from God toward an empty institution of rules, regulations, and rituals.

It's no wonder that an incensed, aggrieved, disgusted Jesus chose aggressive means to cleanse the temple of money changers. He accurately assessed the potential for spiritual harm to those who came to worship and decided that a powerful, no-nonsense statement had to be made. The spiritual welfare of people was at stake, and Jesus loved them, worshippers as well as money changers.

Jesus' behavior in the temple showed the win-lose approach that characterizes aggression: Jesus was determined to win because people's salvation was jeopardized by the Pharisees' emphasis on money, empty ritual, and self-generated righteousness. John 2:13–16 (NIV) tells the story:

> When it was almost time for the Jewish Passover, Jesus went up to Jerusalem. In the temple courts he found men selling cattle, sheep and doves, and others sitting at tables exchanging money. So he made a whip out of cords, and drove all from the temple area, both sheep and cattle; he scattered the coins of the money changers and overturned their tables. To those who sold doves he said, "Get these out of here! How dare you turn my Father's house into a market!"

The same spiritual understanding and insight that caused Jesus to move against the merchants in the temple readied Jesus for frequent and aggressive encounters with the Pharisees. Jesus' motive was not the self-interest one would expect as he meets up with people he knows are plotting to kill him, but instead, the motivation of one who has personally and fully integrated his life's purpose—to secure salvation for all people. Love was always Jesus' motive.

Jesus meant his aggressive remarks to the Pharisees to be shocking. His words were meant to cut into their stone-hard hearts. Jesus purposely chose aggressive means to empower and release the truth of what he was saying. Listen to Jesus address the Pharisees, the shameless, self-serving church leaders of his day:

> "Woe to you, teachers of the law and Pharisees, you hypocrites! You shut the kingdom of heaven in men's faces. You yourselves do not enter, nor will you let those enter who are trying to.

> "Woe to you, teachers of the law and Pharisees, you hypocrites! You travel over land and sea to win a single convert, and when he becomes one, you make him twice as much a son of hell as you are.

> "Woe to you, blind guides! You say, 'If anyone swears by the temple, it means nothing; but if anyone swears by the gold of the temple, he is bound by his oath.' You blind fools! Which is greater: the gold, or the temple that makes the gold sacred? . . .

> "Woe to you, teachers of the law and Pharisees, you hypocrites! You are like whitewashed tombs, which look beautiful on the outside but on the inside are full of dead men's bones and everything unclean" (Matthew 23:13–17, 27 NIV).

Jesus' dealings with the Pharisees demonstrated aggressive behavior, assertively chosen and employed.

Jesus' single-minded attention to his ministry of salvation also led him at times to choose passive instead of aggressive or assertive behavior. When his ministry could be served by choosing passive behaviors, Jesus did so. At times Jesus chose not to take action, not to communicate, not to defend himself, or not to be involved. Far from the under-response of the passive person who is motivated by self-interest or self-preservation, Jesus' passivity was deliberate, goal-oriented, and motivated by love.

When a Samaritan village refused to allow Jesus and his disciples to stay there, Jesus chose not to press the issue, but to go on to another village:

> As the time drew near when Jesus would be taken up to heaven, he made up his mind and set out on his way to Jerusalem. He sent messengers ahead of him, who went into a village in Samaria to get everything ready for him. But the people there would not receive him, because it was clear that he was on his way to Jerusalem. When the disciples James and John saw this, they said, "Lord, do you want us to call fire down from heaven to destroy them?"

> Jesus turned and rebuked them. Then Jesus and his disciples went on to another village (Luke 9:51–56 TEV).

As with his later commissioning of the seventy-two in Luke 10, Jesus invited his followers to choose carefully where they would invest their time, energy, and the power of the gospel. If the people they approached were not welcoming and receptive, Jesus instructed his disciples to refrain from hard-sell, aggressive tactics and from investing their time unprofitably.

Jesus' instructions to his disciples once again underscore the fact that people are free to make choices and that their freedom should be honored. No one can force another to believe, and Jesus indicated that his disciples should, without rancor or hard feelings, use good judgment and go where their message would be received:

> Jesus called his twelve disciples together and gave them authority to drive out evil spirits and to heal every disease and every sickness. . . . These twelve men were sent out by Jesus with the following

instructions: "Do not go to any Gentile territory or any Samaritan towns. Instead, you are to go to those lost sheep, the people of Israel. . . . And if some home or town will not welcome you or listen to you, then leave that place and shake the dust off your feet" (Matthew 10:1, 5–6, 14 TEV).

In order to bring ultimate glory to God and to bring many to faith, Jesus chose not to act immediately when he learned that his dear friend Lazarus was sick. He stayed away from Bethany for two days, until Lazarus died. Jesus chose not to take action so that many would believe that he was the Son of God:

Jesus told them plainly, "Lazarus is dead, but for your sake I am glad that I was not with him, so that you will believe. Let us go to him." . . .

Jesus wept. "See how much he loved him!" the people said.

But some of them said, "He gave sight to the blind man, didn't he? Could he not have kept Lazarus from dying?"

. . . [Jesus] called out in a loud voice, "Lazarus, come out!" He came out, his hands and feet wrapped in grave cloths . . . Many of the people who had come to visit Mary saw what Jesus did, and they believed in him (John 11:14–15, 35–37, 43–45 TEV).

At another time, Jesus chose not to entrust himself to the people in Jerusalem because many were new converts, drawn to Jesus because of the miracles he performed. Even though they acknowledged him to be a teacher come from God, they had to learn that believing was more than seeing signs and being drawn to the one who performed them. Some were still sympathetic spectators, and Jesus chose not to give himself fully to the spectator. He assertively held himself back, reserving a more intimate relationship for his twelve disciples and keeping his own counsel:

While Jesus was in Jerusalem during the Passover Festival, many believed in him as they saw the miracles he performed. But Jesus did not trust himself to them, because he knew them all. There was no need for anyone to tell him about them, because he himself knew what was in their hearts (John 2:23–25 TEV).

At his arrest, Jesus assertively chose not to take action to save himself from being taken prisoner. He allowed Judas to kiss him; he allowed the soldiers to take him prisoner. He allowed others to take aggressive action against him because that would serve and fulfill his ministry of salvation:

Jesus was still speaking when Judas, one of the twelve disciples, arrived. With him was a large crowd armed with swords and clubs and sent by the chief priests and the elders. The traitor had given the crowd a signal: "The man I kiss is the one you want. Arrest him!"

Judas went straight to Jesus and said, "Peace be with you, Teacher," and kissed him.

Jesus answered, "Be quick about it, friend!"

Then they came up, arrested Jesus, and held him tight. . . . "Don't you know that I could call on my Father for help, and at once he would send me more than twelve armies of angels? But in that case, how could the Scriptures come true which say that this is what must happen?" (Matthew 26:47–50, 53–54 TEV).

After his arrest, Jesus chose not to participate in the part of his trial in which lies and false witnesses were brought against him. Jesus chose not to defend himself or counterattack. His silence was eloquent testimony that their lies were not worthy of an answer:

The chief priests and the whole Council tried to find some evidence against Jesus in order to put him to death, but they could not find any. Many witnesses told lies against Jesus, but their stories did not agree. . . .

The High Priest stood up in front of them all and questioned Jesus, "Have you no answer to the accusation they bring against you?"

But Jesus kept quiet and would not say a word (Mark 14:55–56, 60–61 TEV).

Assertive living means choosing how to respond to people and events, and Jesus is the model for assertive Christians. Jesus first chose to love others, and because of that choice his responses are clear examples of the assertive lifestyle. But sometimes, again by assertive choice, Jesus responded aggressively or passively. The key is in the loving and in the choosing.

Love Is an Assertive Force

Jesus was strikingly consistent. He was consistently motivated by love. He knew God and he knew God's will. He knew himself and his ministry, and his entire life moved toward accomplishing one purpose: bringing salvation to all people. His love for all people caused Jesus to make assertive choices throughout his life in order to accomplish his saving purpose.

Even in giving his life, Jesus made it clear that he was no helpless victim, buffeted by the evil, unfairness, and cruelties of life. Jesus was instead God's obedient, willing servant, fully active in God's plan of salvation:

"No one takes my life away from me. I give it up of my own free will. I have the right to give it up, and I have the right to take it back. This is what my Father has commanded me to do" (John 10:18 TEV).

5

Using the Whole Counsel of God

New airplane pilots often have trouble learning to scan a whole panel of instruments at once, Bernie May, former director of the U. S. Division of Wycliffe Bible Translators, explains. Their normal reflex is to concentrate on one thing at a time. Flying, however, demands the ability to do a number of things at the same time. Feet constantly adjust the rudder panels. One hand holds the wheel to keep the plane straight and level. The other hand adjusts throttle, prop, radio, trim, and flaps. Ears tune in the radio, engine—even the sound of the wind. Eyes must not only watch the ground and horizon, but check a lapful of maps and constantly scan the instrument panel.

New pilots must fight the tendency to stare at just one instrument, neglecting all the others. Unless pilots train their eyes to rapidly and repeatedly scan the many instruments before them, they will eventually get into serious trouble.

Christians have a similar problem. Some get preoccupied with certain biblical truths and focus only on them while excluding other important passages. As a result, their spiritual vision gets blurry. When this happens, they risk going into a fatal spin—with their eyes glued to a full fuel gauge, praising God that they're making excellent speed! Christians must learn to scan the whole counsel of God and keep looking at the larger picture of God's revealed will for their lives.

Many Christians have been trained from early childhood to focus on the Bible passages that deal with meekness, submission, and self-denial. And that emphasis is certainly necessary to balance the Old Adam, which Scripture describes as selfish and self-serving, always in opposition to God. But concentrating only on one kind of passage blurs spiritual vision. Christians who do this may find it difficult, for example, to reconcile an oversimplified (and often erroneous) understanding of meekness and submission with an assertive Jesus. When you focus only on passages about humility, your spiritual vision may become too blurred to see the passages that urge you to value yourself as God does, to take hold of your life and be responsible for your choices, and to be bold and courageous as you tell the wonders God has done. If you mistake humility for a kind of self-hate and then read that you are to love your neighbor as you love yourself, the distinct possibility arises that your neighbor will be in big trouble.

As you scan the whole counsel of God, you come to appreciate the complexity of the Christian life, and you can learn to recognize the oversimplified vision that fails to do justice to the richly interwoven, beautifully balanced life God wants you to live.

Assertiveness and Worm Theology

"Worm theology" takes its name and its identity from the well-loved Christian hymn by Isaac Watts, "Alas! And Did My Savior Bleed." The first verse reads:

Alas! and did my Savior bleed,
And did my Sov'reign die?
Would He devote that sacred head
For such a worm as I?

This hymn focuses on a truth familiar to each of us: We realize we are unworthy of God's great love. What a fine and useful discipline it is to pause from time to time to realize that God's love and salvation are a generous, wondrous gift, and that no act we can perform and no change we can make in ourselves will ever make us worthy of such love.

David writes in Psalm 22:6 (NRSV), "I am a worm, and not human" to emphasize his understanding of his lowliness before God. Job 25:6 refers to the individual as "only a worm" (NIV) to point out human inadequacy. Scriptures call Christians to a blessed humility:

No one is respected unless he is humble; arrogant people are on the way to ruin (Proverbs 18:12 TEV).

Is there anyone among you who is wise and understanding? He is to prove it by his good life, by his good deeds performed with humility and wisdom (James 3:13 TEV).

Don't do anything from selfish ambition or from a cheap desire to boast, but be humble toward one another, always considering others better than yourselves (Philippians 2:3 TEV).

As you scan the whole of Scripture, the whole counsel of God, however, you see a very balanced and positive picture of how highly God values people. God has made a bold personal commitment to all people:

"I have written your name on the palms of my hands" (Isaiah 49:16 TEV).

"Before I formed you in the womb I knew you, before you were born I set you apart" (Jeremiah 1:5 NIV).

Even before the world was made, God had already chosen us to be his through our union with Christ (Ephesians 1:4 TEV).

God underscores people's value. The basis of self-esteem is God's esteem for each person.

Assertiveness is compatible with the balance of genuine humility and healthy self-esteem in each person's life. In fact, assertive behavior promotes both humility and self-esteem by creating a healthy tension as Christians strive to honor others as well as themselves.

If, however, you focus only on humility, your vision is

likely to blur with a kind of reverse pride: "See how humble I am." "People should be more humble—like me." Or "I'll never honor myself or say what I want because I am so humble." This blurred vision of misdirected humility may take an equally damaging turn as a person repeatedly and passively defers decisions to others, believing he or she is only exhibiting humility. Others must then make important life choices for the passive person, and both parties may become angry with each other. The passive, inappropriately humble person may become angry because he or she feels powerless. The individual who must always make the decisions becomes angry because he or she may not want so much of the responsibility so much of the time.

Assertiveness helps balance God-pleasing humility with God-pleasing self-esteem so that you honor the rights of others while you honor yourself. Assertiveness can also help you avoid the sins of reverse pride and of shirking your rightful responsibilities, because to be assertive means to be response-able, able to respond to life, able to make choices, able to be strong and capable, because God's power is alive in you.

Assertiveness and Turning the Other Cheek

More confusion has sprung up in the minds of Christians about *turning the other cheek* than almost any other of Jesus' teachings. The phrase is part of the Sermon on the Mount, from a section that strongly contrasts Jesus' ethical teachings with the prevailing Jewish traditions and interpretations of the Old Testament teachings about revenge:

> "You have heard that it was said, 'An eye for an eye, and a tooth for a tooth.' But now I tell you: do not take revenge on someone who wrongs you. If anyone slaps you on the right cheek, let him slap your left cheek too" (Matthew 5:38–39 TEV).

Jesus was rejecting not the Old Testament law, but rather the mindless legalism that had become the emphasis of the church leaders of his day. Jesus repeatedly challenged their distortion of Sabbath law, for example, and forcefully reminded the Pharisees that the Sabbath laws were given to bless and enrich the spiritual lives of people. The Pharisees were insisting that the people focus on the Old Testament laws, making the laws an end in themselves. The predictable results were power struggles, false pride, and the hypocrisy of keeping the laws externally (to supposedly gain merit before God and others) while breaking the laws inwardly.

It is with that background, then, that we hear Jesus saying, "It was said," referring to the Old Testament law that allowed any person who had experienced insult, violence, or injury to inflict similar injuries on the offender:

> "Anyone who commits murder shall be put to death, and anyone who kills an animal belonging to someone else must replace it. The principle is a life for a life.

> "If anyone injures another person, whatever he has done shall be done to him. If he breaks a bone, one of his bones shall be broken; if he puts out an eye, one of his eyes shall be put out; if he knocks out a tooth, one of his teeth shall be knocked out. Whatever injury he causes another person shall be done to him in return" (Leviticus 24:17–20 TEV).

Never intended to incite violence, those Old Testament laws actually functioned to curb and control lawlessness and violent behavior so that people could live peacefully.

Jesus wanted to restore the peace-promoting spirit of the law and to show the law's fullest meaning: "'Do not think that I have come to abolish the law or the prophets; I have come not to abolish but to fulfill'" (Matthew 5:17 NRSV). In this way, Jesus called his people to move beyond the Old Testament laws of revenge to the higher law of love. The law of revenge and retaliation is written in each heart; Jesus challenged his followers to make other choices. He knew the challenge would result in a profound spiritual struggle within each person. And because only the grace of God could produce such character, his followers would need to stay in close relationship with God and use God's resources in order to make such radical changes.

Jesus wasn't telling people to submit passively to physical abuse or to invite physical injury. Rather, he was urging his followers, after one indignity, to be prepared to submit to another without retaliation. For example, working with a difficult person's problems with verbal abuse may require long-term attention, and you may be hurt more than once before the problem is resolved. By assertively setting limits on the amount of abuse that person may inflict on you, you have made a commitment to stay in relationship with that person and to participate in that person's attempts to change unacceptable behavior. You don't support a person's violation of the commandment that says, "'Do not accuse anyone falsely'" (Deuteronomy 5:20 TEV) by ignoring verbal abuse or passively submitting to it. But, as God calls you to obey the law of love, you know that your continued dealings with the verbal abuser may well leave you vulnerable to abuse again.

"Turning the other cheek" isn't a license for abusers, but rather a decision by the abused that could bring hope to an otherwise hopeless situation.

Jesus is asking for an assertive, not a passive, approach to problems of abuse: A decision to leave retribution to God while caring for oneself as well as for the offender. Only the grace of God can produce such character.

Perhaps the best comment on "turning the other cheek" is Jesus' own response to physical abuse, recorded in John 18:19–23 (TEV). When Jesus was illegally slapped by one of the officials at his trial, he didn't turn the other cheek to be slapped again. Instead, he spoke up with an assertive challenge, insisting that the abuser follow the legally proper procedure and testify formally against him:

> The High Priest questioned Jesus about his disciples and about his teaching. Jesus answered, "I have always spoken publicly to everyone; all my teaching

was done in the synagogues and in the Temple, where all the people come together. I have never said anything in secret. Why, then, do you question me? Question the people who heard me. Ask them what I told them—they know what I said."

When Jesus said this, one of the guards there slapped him and said, "How dare you talk like that to the High Priest!"

Jesus answered him, "If I have said anything wrong, tell everyone here what it was. But if I am right in what I have said, why do you hit me?"

Assertiveness and Walking the Extra Mile

"'And if one of the occupation troops forces you to carry his pack one mile, carry it two miles'" (Matthew 5:41 TEV). In this verse Jesus is still speaking the Sermon on the Mount and emphasizing the folly of focusing on the Old Testament laws of retaliation and revenge. The loving behavior that Jesus commands presupposes vindication by God.

In Matthew 5:41, Jesus is referring specifically to the authorization that Caesar's messengers and soldiers were given to commandeer horses, carriages, and even people into their service, by force, when they were needed. Naturally, the people resented this practice and fulfilled such demands unwillingly and angrily. Jesus invited them to make another choice. He invited them to make an assertive decision to comply—for the sake of peace.

Jesus was inviting his followers to live as he himself lived: depending on the strength and power of God for protection in the face of each day's challenges because God ultimately and profoundly protects his people from harm. Jesus' example is described in Scripture: "When he was abused, he did not return abuse; when he suffered, he did not threaten; but he entrusted himself to the one who judges justly" (1 Peter 2:23 NRSV).

Jesus was asking his followers to give up what they had a right to keep, to avoid the quarrelsome and resistive lifestyle, and to live peaceably. St. Paul later wrote to the Christians at Rome:

> If someone has done you wrong, do not repay him with a wrong. Try to do what everyone considers to be good. Do everything possible on your part to live in peace with everybody. Never take revenge, my friends, but instead let God's anger do it. For the scripture says, "I will take revenge, I will pay back, says the Lord." Instead, as the scripture says: "If your enemy is hungry, feed him; if he is thirsty, give him a drink; for by doing this you will make him burn with shame." Do not let evil defeat you; instead, conquer evil with good (Romans 12:17–21 TEV).

St. Paul underscores Jesus' teaching that the response to injustice and evil is to be active, proactive, assertive. Both Jesus and Paul assure you that you can indeed "overcome evil with good." And both suggest that every Christian must make choices and decisions so that his or her behavior will match the belief that God will ultimately right the wrongs done to his people.

Assertiveness and Meekness

"'Blessed are the meek, for they will inherit the earth'" (Matthew 5:5 NIV). This saying is one of the Beatitudes, which describe the qualities of the children of God.

Few words in the Bible are as widely misunderstood as the word *meek*. People described as meek today are generally thought to be any or all of the following: spinelessly submissive, indecisive, easily imposed upon, weak, spiritless, or lacking in self-respect. According to the usual modern understanding, the meek individual is a passive, ineffectual person. It seems strange, then, that Jesus would call such a pitiful, hapless individual "blessed."

What did Jesus mean by the word *meek* when he held up

meekness as a blessed quality for the children of God? Jesus is an assertive, vigorous, active person—would he have asked people to live a lifestyle he himself did not live?

The Hebrew word used in the Old Testament that is translated "meek" is *anaw*, which refers to the person who obediently accepts God's guidance. In the New Testament, the Greek word *praus*, which has been translated "meek," continues the Hebrew meaning of obedience but adds the concept that a meek person isn't quickly or easily angered but knows the right time and the right cause for anger.

Meek, as the word was used and understood in Jesus' time, describes a person not easily provoked to anger, someone who behaves courteously, a person who doesn't envy the gifts and talents of others, someone who is willing to be instructed and admonished, a person who doesn't strive, strain, or overreach for position or status.

Most important is the spiritual dimension of meekness: A meek person is committed to God and waits patiently and quietly for God's help and vindication.

Throughout Scripture *meek, gentle and kind, patient and mild*, and *humble in spirit* are used interchangeably. Jesus is described as "gentle and humble in heart" (Matthew 11:29 NRSV). St. Paul appeals to the Corinthians "by the meekness and gentleness of Christ" (2 Corinthians 10:1 NRSV). Peter describes the beauty of a Christian woman as "the lasting beauty of a gentle and quiet spirit, which is very precious in God's sight" (1 Peter 3:4 NRSV).

The meek are able to show their displeasure (and even anger) without losing control and becoming aggressive. Far from being passive and underresponsive, the meek are well balanced, courteous, respectful, and kind. The patience, kindness, humility, and goodness of the meek Christian are evidence of the Spirit's presence. And the Spirit's presence means power for living—powerful meekness!

Jesus himself shows us that meekness and assertiveness are compatible—indeed, practically identical. Jesus was the very definition of a humble and gentle spirit, and yet Jesus was unmistakably assertive. Jesus' meekness translated into a loving, respectful, infinitely kind regard for all people, a compassionate lifestyle that modeled quiet submission and obedience to God. And yet Jesus was decisive, active, involved, resolute. Jesus took charge, made decisions, and moved single-mindedly toward his goal of salvation for all people. He had an iron will when dealing with demons, a mind of his own when criticized by family and friends, and the courage of his convictions when challenged by the Pharisees.

Jesus beautifully demonstrates assertiveness in his meekness, scanning the needs and demands of each situation, integrating the need for courage and strength with the blessings of yielding to the will of God and serving the needs of others. Jesus avoids the blurred spiritual vision brought on by focusing on either assertiveness or meekness as if they were distinct and separate, instead of rightly blending the two into a personal style that pleases God.

6

Assertive Prayer, Praise, and Admonition

What a blessed obligation Christians have to apply what we know and believe about God to the challenges of living! Surely the Holy Spirit leads us as we live a life that makes an unmistakable statement about what we believe and in whom we believe.

By now you realize that an appropriate amount of assertiveness is necessary to live the Christian life, to decisively, actively, and proactively put faith into practice. Assertiveness helps you as you live in community with your brothers and sisters in Christ and as you live among people who don't yet know Jesus as Savior and Lord.

Scripture repeatedly encourages, commands, warns, and reassures Christians who step up to the challenge of applying their faith to daily living. James gives insight into what it takes to function effectively as a Christian:

> Do not merely listen to the word, and so deceive yourselves. Do what it says. . . . Religion that God our Father accepts as pure and faultless is this: to look after orphans and widows in their distress and to keep oneself from being polluted by the world (James 1:22, 27 NIV).

Being "doers" and not just "hearers" implies active choice, proactive living, and assertive relationships with God, other believers, and those who don't yet believe. Christians can apply assertiveness to everyday life in many distinctively Christian ways. This chapter examines three of those opportunities: assertive prayer, assertive praise and thanksgiving, and Christian admonition.

Assertive Prayer

A grandmother told the story of overhearing young Carl, her seven-year-old grandson, talking to his friend Aaron. They were playing in the family room and didn't know that the door was open.

Carl's parents had just given him a puppy, and Aaron was complaining because his folks wouldn't allow him to have a dog. "They won't let me have a puppy," he said. "I've begged and begged, and they always say no."

Carl leaned close to give some advice. "You just didn't go about it in the right way. You keep asking for a *puppy*. The best way to get a puppy is to beg for a baby brother—and they'll settle for a puppy every time!"

Unlike young Carl, who worked out a clever but manipulative way to get a puppy, Christians bring their prayer requests to God in response to God's own invitation to pray assertively. God invites you to pray with a direct, candid, and open spirit. No games, no deals, no hidden agendas.

Assertive prayer requests are characterized by at least two important elements: Ask boldly and confidently, and then act on the answer God gives.

Ask Boldly and Confidently

As you present your prayer requests to God, you can ask boldly, confident that God cares deeply for you. Paul describes the depth of God's love to the Christians at Rome in Romans 5:6–8, 10–11 (TEV):

> For when we were still helpless, Christ died for the wicked at the time that God chose. It is a difficult thing for someone to die for a righteous person. It may even be that someone might dare to die for a good person. But God has shown us how much he loves us—it was while we were still sinners that Christ died for us! . . . We were God's enemies, but he made us his friends through the death of his Son.

Now that we are God's friends, how much more will we be saved by Christ's life! But that is not all; we rejoice because of what God has done through our Lord Jesus Christ, who has now made us God's friends.

God's commitment to you transcends your helplessness and reaches past the ugliness of your sin to change you from an enemy into a friend. God took the initiative to save you because you were helpless to save yourself.

Paul explains to the Romans that God operates above and beyond the criteria people might use to determine whether lifesaving heroics are in order: How good is this person? Is this person worth the sacrifice of my life? While people may weigh a recipient's worthiness before making a sacrifice, God loved us so much that he chose us while we were unworthy and unlovable. That kind of grace sets the tone for bold and confident prayers to a God who would go to such lengths to save his people and shower them with every blessing.

In Romans 8:14–17 (TEV), Paul writes:

Those who are led by God's Spirit are God's sons. For the Spirit that God has given you does not make you slaves and cause you to be afraid; instead, the Spirit makes you God's children, and by the Spirit's power we cry out to God, "Father! my Father!" God's Spirit joins himself to our spirits to declare that we are God's children. Since we are his children, we will possess the blessings he keeps for his people, and we will also possess with Christ what God has kept for him; for if we share Christ's suffering, we will also share his glory.

What a blessed word from God! God adopts as sons and daughters those who believe in the Son of God and gives them the Spirit to take away their fear. No longer slaves but heirs, no longer afraid but courageous, no longer reticent but empowered by the Spirit to cry out to God, "Father! my

Father!" Christians are not afraid to bring their requests assertively to God.

The God who has chosen you to be his own child has promised to hear your prayers. Jesus used a parable to teach his disciples that they should pray assertively and not become discouraged. The parable is meant to be a study in contrasts. Compare the way the unjust, uncaring judge dealt with the persistent woman, who in the end had to wear down the judge to receive the justice she deserved, with the way our just and loving God readily, willingly hears and answers prayers.

> "In a certain town there was a judge who neither feared God nor respected man. And there was a widow in that same town who kept coming to him and pleading for her rights, saying, 'Help me against my opponent!' For a long time the judge refused to act, but at last he said to himself, 'Even though I don't fear God or respect man, yet because of all the trouble this widow is giving me, I will see to it that she gets her rights. If I don't, she will keep on coming and finally wear me out!'" (Luke 18:2–5 TEV).

Following the parable, Jesus emphasizes that God is responsive and tenderhearted when his children pray:

> And the Lord continued, "Listen to what that corrupt judge said. Now, will God not judge in favor of his own people who cry to him day and night for help? Will he be slow to help them? I tell you, he will judge in their favor and do it quickly" (Luke 18:6–8 TEV).

Christians may assertively bring their prayer requests to God with all boldness and confidence because the same God who in Jesus met their need for salvation has adopted them as dear children and promises to hear and answer their prayers. You may pray assertively, boldly, confidently.

Act on the Answer to Prayer

The story of Peter's walk on water demonstrates the second principle of assertive prayer: Act on the answer to prayer. Matthew tells the story:

> During the fourth watch of the night Jesus went out to them, walking on the lake. When the disciples saw him walking on the lake, they were terrified. "It's a ghost," they said, and cried out in fear.
>
> But Jesus immediately said to them: "Take courage! It is I. Don't be afraid."
>
> "Lord, if it's you," Peter replied, "tell me to come to you on the water."
>
> "Come," he said.
>
> Then Peter got down out of the boat, walked on the water and came toward Jesus (Matthew 14:25–29 NIV).

God's response to your request demands a response from you, an appropriate action. If the answer to your prayer is yes, as it was with Peter, you are to take the next appropriate step. If the answer to your prayer is no, you may need to make an assertive decision to patiently wait, to abandon your request, to submit it another time, or to search for an alternative. When the answer to your prayer request is wait, you can choose to wait assertively and to trust God for the proper timing. Making an assertive choice to act or not to act is the logical next step after boldly making prayer requests in confident dependence on God.

Jesus prayed assertively in the Garden of Gethsemane on the night he was betrayed. Matthew 26:39 records Jesus' bold and candid request that God take the cup of suffering from him. In Luke's account of that evening, Jesus' praying is described as so intense, so bold, and so earnest that "his sweat was like drops of blood falling to the ground" (Luke 22:44 NIV).

Even as Jesus had dared to present his thoughts and feelings assertively and honestly to God and ask that he be spared the terrible suffering that lay ahead, he coupled that request with a witness to his confident dependence on the goodness of the will of God: "'Yet not as I will, but as you will'" (Matthew 26:39 NIV). Jesus made an assertive request and then assertively chose to submit to God's will, whether or not the request was granted.

Jesus prayed persistently, assertively, and courageously three times that night in the garden (Matthew 26:44). And then he roused his disciples and prepared to act on the answer to his prayer. "'Rise, let us go! Here comes my betrayer!'" (Matthew 26:46 NIV).

Jesus knew the will of God for his life and death, accepted the confirmation of that will as he prayed in the garden, and then courageously acted on what he knew and believed was God's will. "I will suffer" is the result of that evening of prayer in Gethsemane, and because Jesus chose to ask boldly, submit confidently, and act courageously, your salvation is assured: "[Jesus] said, 'Here I am, I have come to do your will.'. . . And by that will, we have been made holy" (Hebrews 10:9–10 NIV).

Assertive Praise and Thanksgiving

St. Paul begins his letter to the Christians at Ephesus with a resounding hymn of praise and thanksgiving:

> Praise be to the God and Father of our Lord Jesus Christ, who has blessed us in the heavenly realms with every spiritual blessing in Christ. For he chose us in him before the creation of the world to be holy and blameless in his sight. In love he predestined us to be adopted as his sons through Jesus Christ, in accordance with his pleasure and will—to the praise of his glorious grace, which he has freely given us in the One he loves (Ephesians 1:3–6 NIV).

Paul spans the canopy of time—from time before the world began to the present—to point out why God is worthy of praise. A significant part of Paul's leadership was to lead the early Christians in praise and thanksgiving. As a deliberate act, assertively chosen and acted upon, Paul begins each letter with praise and liberally includes praise and thanksgiving throughout the text of his letters to the early Christian churches.

Praise and thanksgiving are sometimes recorded in the Bible as grateful responses to a wonderful deed or miracle, such as the song of Moses and Miriam after God's spectacular victory over the Egyptians at the crossing of the Red Sea (Exodus 15), or the praise joyfully offered by a whole crowd of disciples on the first Palm Sunday because of "all the miracles they had seen" (Luke 19:37 NIV). Praise and thanksgiving can also be the assertive expression of a happy feeling, as James indicates: "Is anyone happy? Let him sing songs of praise" (James 5:13 NIV). A certain amount of assertiveness is necessary to express praise and thanksgiving, to bring to the surface the thanks and joy you may feel inside.

Praising God is a response not only to good times and happy feelings but also to the revelation of miracles and the bursting forth of hope. Praise and thanksgiving are also to be the outward evidence of an assertive, faith-based decision to praise God no matter what the circumstance. Psalm 42 is a prayer for deliverance from an enemy who has oppressed and crushed the Israelites. Far from just sitting back and remembering God's faithfulness and loving care, the psalmist resolves to actively remember God's goodness by praising God, even in the midst of despair and oppression.

Such active remembering is an assertive, proactive choice that originates in the psalmist's decision to believe in God's goodness and faithfulness, even though he couldn't see it in his dismal circumstance. Assertiveness builds faith by encouraging Christians to act on what they believe, to declare and affirm what it is they believe about God. An assertive Christian praises God for who God is rather than for what God has done. That the praise of the psalmist is a decision and not a response to some good fortune is evident not only in the context but also in the language the writer chooses: "I *will* yet praise him, my Savior and my God" (Psalm 42:11 NIV, emphasis added).

Paul and Silas made a decision to praise God after being attacked by an angry crowd, denied a trial, severely beaten, and then thrown into prison where their feet were fastened in stocks. Acts 16:25 (NIV) recounts: "About midnight Paul and Silas were praying and singing hymns to God, and the other prisoners were listening to them." After such a woeful day, Paul and Silas probably couldn't depend on their natural emotional response to motivate them to praise God. It was by faith that they behaved assertively and decided to praise God, regardless of circumstance or emotional state.

As Paul wrote to the Thessalonians, he put into words the decisive, assertive nature of a Christian's praise: "Be joyful always; pray continually; give thanks in all circumstances, for this is God's will for you in Christ Jesus" (1 Thessalonians 5:16–18 NIV).

Christian Admonition

Few opportunities in Christian living are as neglected as the New Testament directive to "admonish" a Christian brother or sister. What is admonition? How is it practiced? And what does it have to do with assertiveness?

To *admonish* is to "warn against specific faults." Christians have an opportunity to love, support, and minister to other Christians by admonishing a Christian brother or sister caught in a sin. St. Paul explains:

> Brothers, if someone is caught in a sin, you who are spiritual should restore him gently. But watch yourself, or you also may be tempted (Galatians 6:1 NIV).

St. Paul states that if a Christian is aware of a brother or sister who is engaged in open sin, who is endangering his or her salvation, the Christian is to warn that person in a kind and loving manner. But Paul is also quick to caution the admonishing Christian that the one who admonishes faces a particular temptation to sin: the sin of puffed-up pride, the sin of a holier-than-thou attitude, the sin of approaching the brother or sister with an aggressive stance that will wound and harm.

The goal of Christian admonition is to help the brother or sister restore his or her healthy relationship with God and to give the person an opportunity to make new choices that will lead to spiritual wholeness and full life. Within the context of a loving, supportive, encouraging relationship, Christians can confess sin, share forgiveness, and, by the power of the Holy Spirit, make new choices for the future.

Christian admonition is accomplished by following the biblical principle of dealing directly, privately, personally, and confidentially with the person who may need a warning. Matthew 18:15 (NRSV) instructs: "'If another member of the church sins against you, go and point out the fault when the two of you are alone. If the member listens to you, you have regained that one.'" And when you admonish a fellow Christian, you are to listen carefully, prayerfully desiring to serve the spiritual welfare of the other. Christian admonition has no place for a judgmental spirit or harsh words of condemnation because the goal of admonition is restoration.

As St. Paul instructs the Ephesians in community living, he paints an appealing picture of the attitudes Christians should have toward each other: "Be completely humble and gentle; be patient, bearing with one another in love. Make every effort to keep the unity of the Spirit through the bond of peace" (Ephesians 4:2–3 NIV). His later injunction to "[speak] the truth in a spirit of love" (Ephesians 4:15 TEV) fits into the picture of a loving, truthful, assertive Christian community. While a Christian has a duty to admonish, warn, and bring to another Christian's attention a spiritual danger, he or she must prayerfully intend and carefully enact that admonishment. The Christian must have such genuine love that the admonished person will not only be encouraged to listen but also will be inspired by the Holy Spirit to make the necessary life changes.

The practice of Christian admonition demands assertiveness. An assertive Christian who admonishes another Christian will show honest, direct, and natural concern when speaking to the other person. A passive person, on the other hand, might decide to ignore another's spiritual danger; an aggressive person might attack the other person in a cruel or insensitive manner. Loving, assertive directness also contrasts with the attitude of a person who behaves in a passive-aggressive manner, perhaps making jokes or snide remarks to try to draw the person into a conversation about his or her behavior. The direct kindness of a respectful, assertive approach increases the likelihood that the other person will actually hear the concern and understand the warning.

Assertiveness is also essential in a ministry of admonition because such behavior is mutually respectful. Christians who approach others with a warning are respecting themselves because they are taking seriously what the Bible says about admonishing other members of the body. And assertive Christians also respect the person who is being admonished; they won't try to force agreement or manipulate behavior change. They accept their own limitations and know that others are ultimately responsible for their own choices and behaviors.

God offers the ministry of Christian admonition to the Christian community in order to serve, strengthen, and support each member of that community. Those who are in spiritual danger are invited to move toward restoration and spiritual wholeness. Assertive behavior will undergird and support such ministry because assertion skills are the very skills required for dealing openly and honestly with others, especially in sensitive situations. Assertive behavior is nonthreatening and reduces the need for defensive behavior on the part of the one who is being warned. The assertive, loving Christian has the motivation and the communication skills to admonish another Christian in a way that increases the likelihood that he or she will be heard.

The ministry of the person who admonishes is to warn gently, to encourage, and to show patience. St. Paul calls the Christian community to live in peace, as members of one body, even as members accept some responsibility for one another's spiritual welfare:

Let the peace of Christ rule in your hearts, since as members of one body you were called to peace. And be thankful. Let the word of Christ dwell in you richly as you teach and admonish one another with all wisdom, and as you sing psalms, hymns and spiritual songs with gratitude in your hearts to God (Colossians 3:15–16 NIV).

A ministry of admonition is an opportunity to see the power of God at work through the Word and through the love of fellow Christians.

Assertion skills serve the individual Christian as well as the whole Christian community. Whether making prayer requests, decisively choosing to praise God in every circumstance, or lovingly warning another believer who is in spiritual danger, the assertive Christian uses his or her skills effectively to build up the Body of Christ.

PART THREE

Techniques of
Assertiveness

7

Deciding If, When, and Where to Be Assertive

It isn't that I mind being asked; I just mind being asked so often, Frank thought. And people seem to take my willingness for granted. I really want to be helpful, but I don't think I can relay messages accurately, take care of the kids, keep our hectic Sunday schedule, and still be as pleasant as I want to be to all these people. I'm on overload!

Frank could feel his face burning with confusion and annoyance as he struggled to get his daughter Jamie into her snowsuit. Kevin wanted to argue about whether he had to wear his boots, and Kelly still hadn't come up from the basement Sunday school rooms; he would probably have to go downstairs with the unwelcome message that it was time to leave her friends and go home.

Frank is a clergy spouse, the husband of the Rev. Barbara McGuire, and his dilemma concerns his role in relaying messages from congregation members to their pastor, his wife.

Good-natured, well-meaning folks often stop Frank after church on Sunday and say, "I don't want to bother Barbara, but would you tell her that my husband is going into the hospital for a heart catheterization on Tuesday? We'd appreciate her visit, if she has time." Or "Would you ask Rev. McGuire to pray for my son and his wife? They're trying to decide whether or not to enter the mission field." Today someone said to Frank, "Tell Pastor McGuire that I'm not going to be at the elders' meeting Wednesday night. My grandson is seriously ill in Indiana, and we're going there to see if we can help."

Frank's dilemma is especially confusing to him because in his work at the advertising agency he knows intuitively how to assess situations and is comfortable responding assertively. He just doesn't know what to do when he's faced with the need to be assertive about issues concerning Barbara's work. After all, he reasons, this is the church, and these are important personal concerns—concerns that he cares deeply about, too.

Frank's problem isn't a matter of not caring or of petty annoyance at being asked to relay a message. It's a very practical concern: How can he remember each message, keep all the facts and dates and names straight, and still carry out his responsibility for their three children? He and Barbara agreed he would assume primary responsibility for their children each Sunday morning because on Sundays Barbara conducts services, teaches adult class, and gives personal attention to as many members as possible.

Three weeks ago, Frank forgot to tell Barbara about a member's elective surgery, and Barbara had a hurt and angry family on her hands who wondered why she didn't come to the hospital to visit. Once Frank carried a message from a tearful woman who wanted to cancel a counseling appointment with Barbara. Of course, not knowing the confidential details of the woman's need for counseling, Frank was shocked and worried when he told Barbara and she, with some alarm, quickly phoned the woman to check on her. Frank didn't know that the woman had been seriously depressed the week before.

Frank can identify some of the factors that make his situation complex. He feels overwhelmed at trying to care for his children while also trying to receive and relay accurate, detailed messages from members. He's afraid that he might unwittingly hurt someone by forgetting or confusing a message. He's honored that members trust him with their important personal messages, and yet he's becoming a bit annoyed because most people simply assume he'll be able to carry their message to Barbara. They assume that Frank has only one message to carry—theirs. Frank really doesn't mind carrying messages, he simply has too many to remember.

Frank struggled with inner confusion as he pulled mittens on hands and boots on the feet of each of his children. "What is the loving, Christian thing to do in such a sensitive situation?" he wondered.

Frank genuinely wants to serve, but he needs to find a way to balance his love for the church's members with his own personal limitations. There is only one Frank, there are hundreds of members, and he has three children and a wife who depend on him.

Frank wants to behave more assertively, but he's not sure that assertive behavior is appropriate in this situation. And he's not at all sure when or how he can address the problem without offending or giving the impression that he doesn't care about the church members. Frank needs some guidance as he assesses his situation and comes to a decision about what, if anything, to do. Frank needs to define his problem and assess the best time and place to work on it. And, after making a realistic assessment of his chances for even minimal success, he must then decide if he is willing to invest time and energy and endure some risk and anxiety as he changes to new, assertive, more productive behaviors.

Assertive Christians realize that not every problem has to be solved, not every issue has to be addressed, not every situation must be approached assertively. Assessing a situation requires careful thought and a willingness to be scrupulously honest. Here are five questions you might ask in order to assess a situation and decide if, when, and how to adopt a more assertive approach.

1. Is this a problem (and how do I know if it's a problem)?

Is it a problem or just an inconvenience or something that's not to your liking? Does the problem cause you more than just a mild annoyance? Pay attention to your feelings about the situation. You can usually determine how honestly dissatisfied you are, especially in situations that happen repeatedly, like Frank McGuire's dilemma.

For example, Arlene could tell she had a problem with the way she dealt with the parents of her fourth graders because when she conducted parent-teacher conferences, she usually felt painfully inadequate and deeply disappointed. What she wanted was to form a working partnership with each of the parents. She could tell she wasn't accomplishing that, however, because the parents told her they didn't know how to help their children with the assignments she sent home.

She thought she would come closer to achieving a partnership if she could behave more assertively when she met with the parents. Behaving assertively would include giving parents very specific instructions and feedback on the homework assignments, hints about how to work with their children, and suggestions for fun at-home activities involving children and parents. She wanted to speak up and take charge in an appropriate and helpful way.

Beware: Well-meaning, loving Christians are sometimes tempted to deny the existence or the seriousness of a real problem and to minimize the feelings they have about the problem. Sometimes they passively pretend, "It doesn't matter," or "I don't care," or "It's really okay with me," when it does matter and they do care and it's not really okay.

Often you can decide whether or not you have a problem by thinking about your goals and asking if the way you're now behaving helps you reach those goals. For example, if Frank McGuire's goals were to carefully attend to his children on Sunday mornings, to assist his wife by relaying accurate messages in a timely fashion, and to convey his own personal love and concern for the church members, he wasn't meeting all his goals. Frank assessed that he had a problem and that his current behavior wasn't helping to solve that problem.

Besides your own feelings and your awareness of whether or not you're meeting your goals, the possibility that someone else might be hurt is another indication that a problem needs to be addressed. For example, Frank

McGuire was well aware of the potential for harm should he forget a message or confuse names and dates.

At times you'll decide to choose more assertive behavior because remaining passive could be harmful to others and behaving assertively would be the loving, Christian, responsible thing to do. For years Sarah distanced herself from people who were wheelchair-bound. She decided to change from passive to assertive behavior, however, when she volunteered to work one Saturday morning at a health fair booth and found herself paired with Barbara, another volunteer, who was in a wheelchair. As Sarah and Barbara talked that morning, Sarah came to realize that she usually acted passively when she was around a person in a wheelchair, looking the other way or unintentionally ignoring the person. Now Sarah wants to behave more assertively because she understands that assertive, respectful behavior is loving, responsible behavior.

2. Is this the time and place?

If you've decided that the situation you're facing is indeed a problem for you, the second question to ask is whether this is the best time and the best place to address the problem. Some problems need to be addressed immediately and publicly while other problems are best approached with careful timing and great sensitivity.

For example, when Jan realized that her teenage daughter Sally was borrowing her clothes without permission, she decided to wait to confront her until Sally's friends, who were staying overnight, had gone home. Earlier that same day, however, Jan found it necessary to respond immediately to coworkers' sexist remarks during a meeting at her office. She wisely allowed no time to lapse between the offense and her response, letting the offenders know that their remarks merited an immediate response. And, because their remarks were made publicly, she decided to respond publicly and assertively, without aggression or abuse.

It's also important to determine the proper arena in which to deal assertively with a problem. In many cases, in order to have mutually respectful relationships with others, you'll choose a place in which both parties feel comfortable, probably a private place with few distractions where you can easily be heard and where you can listen most attentively to the other.

3. *What are my chances of at least a small measure of success initially?*

Most important problems are not solved quickly, easily, or completely. In assessing an issue, you can mentally measure how close your first assertive step might bring you to your overall goal for the situation.

For example, Tim decided to assert himself with a brother-in-law who frequently teased him about his thinning hair. Because his brother-in-law had been making insensitive and teasing remarks for several years and Tim had never complained, Tim knew it would probably take a while for Jack to realize that Tim was painfully sensitive to his remarks. Because Tim assessed that Jack was not intentionally being malicious, he thought he would be likely to have some measure of success with his first request.

Beware: If the problem is important to you, you might be tempted to "catastrophize" and tell yourself things like "He'll never listen to me," or "She'll never change," or "This won't do any good." Resist that temptation, gather up your courage, and take at least a small step toward your goal.

4. *Am I willing to invest time and energy and to endure some risk in order to make the change?*

Changing from nonproductive or counterproductive behaviors to behaviors that genuinely enhance relationships requires time, energy, great thoughtfulness, and a purposeful investment of self.

You can't change another person's behavior; you have to change your own behavior and hope that the other might change in response to your change. When you deliver unexpected messages and upset the careful balances you've already established in your relationships, you're taking a risk. Assess early on whether the risk is worth the reward of increased self-esteem, enhanced and enriched relationships, and increased mutual respect. Many people count the cost and courageously decide to assert themselves. Usually they're not disappointed.

5. *Will I stay relatively calm while I try some new
    behaviors, not letting fears or anxieties overwhelm me?*

Think about and assess your anxiety level before deciding to make an important change. Stress accompanies all change, so you can expect some discomfort and stress when you attempt to replace passive or aggressive behaviors with assertive behaviors. You may also have to cope with fear—fear of others' reactions to your new behavior, fear of the unknown, fear of losing the approval of people important to you.

Weigh the emotional discomfort (which is temporary) associated with change against the potential for a new, healthy balance and the genuine pleasure of mutual respect (which can be lasting). Even though there is no perfect solution to any problem, many people decide to try a new, assertive approach to a problem, believing that the potential gain will outweigh the potential pain.

8

What to *Say* When You Want to Be Assertive

Andy and Claire Greenwald were excited. The house next door had finally sold and now they had new neighbors. But what was most exciting was that they had heard from the real estate agent that the Barneses were about their age and had two boys, just their own sons' ages. Andy and Claire welcomed the thought of neighbors with so much in common and couldn't help but hope that they would all become good friends.

They remembered all too well the complaints of the previous owners who thought the boys made too much noise playing in the backyard and who phoned in annoyance whenever the boys' ball went over the fence into their yard. Andy and Claire had tried their best to be good neighbors, but now they hoped for a more mutual relationship with their new neighbors.

The Greenwalds were also feeling apprehensive. How could they best introduce themselves, and what would be the right way to let the Barnes family know just how glad they were that they were going to be neighbors?

So Andy and Claire stood at their living room window and watched the movers unload their new neighbors' furniture, trying to decide what to do and what to say.

Whenever you, like the Greenwalds, have the opportunity to move assertively into a potentially positive experience or are faced with the need to address a problem assertively, the following guidelines for assertive speech can help you communicate directly, honestly, and effectively.

Say Something

First of all, you need to *say something!* Don't wait until you have the perfect opening. Some people wait for years to think of the perfect opening instead of asserting themselves and speaking out. Remember, it's less important that you say the perfect words than that you move ahead, speak out, and assert yourself.

Be Honest

Say exactly what you want and need to say to get your point across. Be honest. If you equivocate or if you disguise what you really want to say, you'll give others a confusing or less-than-truthful answer.

For example, you and a friend are going out to dinner. The friend suggests, "Let's try that new Italian restaurant."

You don't like Italian food, but you say instead, "Isn't it too far out of the way?" Of course, what you really want to say is that you don't want to go to an Italian restaurant. But unless your friend can read your mind, he or she probably won't know this and might respond, "Oh, we can be there in 15 minutes," or "Okay, let's go to Tony's Italian Spaghetti House instead. That's closer."

You could have said, "No, I don't like Italian food that much. How about some other restaurant?" Then you and your friend could have easily picked out a mutually agreeable place to eat.

Use "I" Messages

Using "I" messages assertively communicates your feelings to another. The primary characteristic of an I message is using the word *I*, showing that you own or are responsible for your statement. Here are some examples of I messages:

"I felt hurt when you didn't call me back last night like you said you would."

"I'm really happy you can come to visit with us."
"I feel really good because we can spend our day off together."

Each of these examples also expresses a feeling and explains why you feel the way you do.

Use "I Want" Statements

An "I want" statement is similar to an I message. An I want statement contains the word *I* and a specific request about the behavior you'd like to see happen. Here are some examples of I want messages:

"I want you to stop teasing your sister."
"I'd rather go to a movie instead of a play."
"I want you to sit down and listen to me."

Combine I Want Statements and I Messages

Sometimes you'll combine an I message and an I want statement, as in a situation where you're expressing anger to someone and then requesting that the person change the behavior that you feel angry about. For example:

"I get annoyed when you use the telephone almost constantly from right after supper until nearly 10 P.M. In the future, I'd like you not to tie up the phone line from 6:30 to 8:00 so I can make and receive phone calls during that time."

Here's another situation: A woman is working hard to clean up the home. She needs some help from her husband and is angry that he said he wants to watch a football game instead. What should she say to express herself?

Don't Say: "If you really loved me and were a good husband, you'd pitch in and help me."

Do Say: "I'm upset that you're sitting there relaxing while

I'm doing all this work. I'd really like you to do part of the housework this afternoon."

In the Don't Say example, the woman used the subject "you" instead of "I," failed to express her feelings, and tried to manipulate her husband into helping her by implying that if he didn't help her, he didn't love her. A better way to make this request is in the Do Say example, where she accepts ownership for her feelings and makes a direct request of her husband.

Avoid Labeling

Critical labeling does absolutely no good; it invites the other person to feel attacked and then behave defensively. Labeling the person prevents you from owning your feelings and can easily lead to verbal attacks on the other person. Instead, identify the behavior or the specific actions to which you're reacting. Using I messages and I want statements can help you avoid labeling. For example:

Don't Say: "You're really lazy. I don't understand how you can let the grass get so long before you mow it."

Do Say: "I'm very irritated that you still haven't mowed the grass because it makes our yard look shabby. Could you please mow it before our guests arrive."

Note that in the Don't Say example, the person aggressively responded to the situation, labeling the person as lazy. But in the Do Say example, the person assertively responded to the situation, not by labeling, but by describing the objectionable behavior. In the Do Say example, the person expressed feelings clearly without attacking the other person.

This guideline also applies when you want to express affectionate feelings or appreciation. In such instances, assertive statements avoid labeling the person. For example:

Don't Say: "You're such a nice person."

Do Say: "I'm glad you stopped by to see how I'm doing, and I really appreciate your taking the time."

Note that in the Don't Say example, the person was labeled in a very general way. Express this compliment better by describing the specific behavior or action you appreciated—in this case the other person's visit.

Be Concise

When you assertively communicate with others, you don't need to lecture or offer long-winded explanations. People respect and respond to messages that are to the point. When asserting yourself, be relatively brief. For example:

Don't Say: "Well, I don't know if I can go or not. You know how it is on the weekends. I guess everybody's busy on weekends, but I think this is going to be one of the worst. There are so many things to do around the house, and I have been saying to myself that I have to catch up on everything. Especially since I was sick last week. I had the flu for two days; I just seem to get every one of those bugs that goes around. I was out of commission for two days and you know how that can take the middle out of a week. I don't think I'll ever catch up. But I'm going to try this weekend. Besides that, we've got old friends from Philadelphia coming over on Saturday. They used to live next door to us when we were in that row house. They really love plants, and so I've got to get a few flowers in the flower boxes, too. I know they would enjoy that. Of course, I'm already late with all the planting, too, so it's just going to be rush, rush, rush this weekend. Wow! Makes me tired just thinking about it all. Wish I could go with you, but I just can't."

Do Say: "Thanks for asking me to go with you, but I have a full weekend already. I've got a lot of catching up to do because I was sick this week. And we've got some old friends coming to town on Saturday. We always enjoy the time we spend with you, so let's plan on another time."

Don't Apologize for Asserting Yourself

You don't need to feel sorry or apologetic when you've asserted yourself legitimately, appropriately, and respectfully. For example:

Don't Say: "I'm sorry I have to bring this to your attention. I don't mean to be hard to get along with, but you failed to finish the work you promised to do on the roof of our house."

Do Say: "You said you'd finish the work on our roof by last Friday and it still isn't finished. I'd like you to finish it today."

You don't have to justify your feelings, whine, or plead with people. Those responses are passive, not assertive.

Avoid Sarcasm

Avoid being sarcastic in your responses. Sarcasm is always aggressive! It belittles others' actions, hides your true feelings, and prevents constructive communication. For example: You want to buy a book and the salesperson is obviously ignoring you. After chatting with other clerks for several minutes while you wait, the salesperson comes over to help you without apologizing for the delay.

Don't Say (pretending to smile innocently): "Oh, are you sure you're not too busy to wait on me? I can wait all day, you know."

Do Say: "I'm unhappy that I had to wait several minutes before you came to wait on me. I'd appreciate prompt service."

Be As Persistent As Necessary

Sometimes you may need to use an I message or an I want statement more than once. For example, you're returning a sweater that shrank to a department store, and you want a refund. The clerk asks if you followed the manufacturer's directions for laundering the item, and you assure her that you did.

You: "This sweater shrank even though I followed the washing directions carefully. I'd like my money back."

Clerk: "Have you seen the new sweaters we just got in? Maybe you'd like to exchange this for one of those."

You: "No, thanks. I just want a refund."

Clerk: "We haven't had any other sweaters like this returned; maybe you just got a bad one. We still have some in your size. Do you want to try again?"

You: "No, I don't want another sweater. I'd just appreciate having my money back."

A gentle but firm persistence eventually focuses attention on your I want statements and I messages and increases the possibility that you'll be heard and your request will be considered.

If people could read one another's minds, they wouldn't need to work so hard at communicating. But people need to depend on what they say to one another to communicate their thoughts, feelings, and expectations. If you're willing to make a real effort to learn to communicate assertively—in an honest, simple, straightforward manner—you'll be better able to help people understand what you want to say. The results are definitely worth the effort.

9

What to *Do* When You Want to Be Assertive

"You people aren't taking me seriously! What do I have to do to make you believe that I mean what I say? In my last report I said that I had the Thomasville job under control. I told you that I would get to the bottom of the contractor's delays, activate the penalties in the contract, and find a new jobber if necessary. Now I find out that you've asked Sharon to see what's going on out at the Thomasville job! What do I have to do to get you to take me seriously?"

Julie hated losing her temper and she hated her outburst of frustration and anger, but she felt helpless and ineffective. She had been working diligently for eight months to change from a passive, quiet person to someone who could speak up, appropriately express her opinions, and make significant recommendations at the office. She knew that in the past she'd been overly concerned about pleasing people, worried about whether or not others liked her, and especially mindful of appearing to be a happy, cheerful Christian in the workplace.

As Julie came to realize that she needed a more honest, balanced presentation of herself to others, she had studied assertiveness and had been making steady progress, working to change her passive style of relating to people that was designed to please and placate to a more honest, straightforward, assertive style.

What puzzled Julie most was that she knew she had made significant progress in becoming more assertive. For example, in the past she had let others pile her desk with work and impose arbitrary and inconvenient deadlines so that she had to work overtime several nights each week.

Julie had developed an assertive style and a workable system that had eliminated all but the most necessary overtime, and she felt good about it. And, no longer paralyzed with fear and insecurity, she was starting to volunteer ideas and offer solutions to office problems presented at the weekly staff meetings. Many of her ideas had been accepted and used successfully. Julie knew she was making progress in learning to speak and act more assertively.

Still Julie wondered and stewed. She knew she could deal effectively with the Thomasville problems. But obviously the others had their doubts. Was something in her manner or personal style causing a credibility gap?

The words a person says are only part of a communication; the real impact of a message comes from body language and the way the message sounds to others. You may have all the right words, plus the ideas and philosophy to undergird them and a host of experts to back you, but if your body language says you're unsure and your voice wavers in indecision, your listeners may be confused and uncertain about how valid and credible your words are.

People receive an entire communication, both verbal and nonverbal, at one time. If the verbal and nonverbal messages aren't consistent with each other, listeners will believe the nonverbal message more readily than the verbal message. That was Julie's problem. She still gave the impression that she was unsure of herself, and her coworkers picked it up in her hesitant speech, poor eye contact, and the almost constant smile that betrayed her great need for approval from others. Julie was indeed learning to be assertive, and she was making encouraging progress. But Julie had yet to learn the importance of her nonverbal communication. Julie can learn to strengthen her assertive verbal messages and greatly enhance their effectiveness by combining them with assertive nonverbal messages.

Here are some suggestions that will assure your nonverbal messages are assertive.

Look the Way You Feel

Match your facial expressions with your words. If you're happy, look happy when you speak. If you're angry, don't smile when you express your anger. Many people wear a smile when they're expressing anger because they hope to soften the effect of their anger and avoid alienating the other person. They usually so confuse the listener that the impact of the anger message is lost and the listener fails to take the speaker seriously.

Use Assertive Gestures

Use gestures that flow naturally from your assertive statements. Avoid aggressive gestures such as a clenched fist or pointed fingers; likewise avoid passive gestures such as wringing your hands, fidgeting, and jingling coins or keys.

Speak Clearly

Speak plainly and clearly. Let your voice reflect your assertive behavior. Avoid mumbling or speaking in a monotone that hides what you want to say. If what you say requires raising your voice, do so, but avoid losing control, yelling, or aggressively intimidating the other person. Threatening others is no part of assertive behavior.

Face the Person

Look at the person, and perhaps lean a bit toward him or her. This makes it obvious that you're speaking to the person; it also draws his or her attention toward you and what you are communicating.

Maintain Eye Contact

Assertive eye contact is comfortably direct. Look at the person to show that you're interested, that you'll pay attention to his or her reactions as you speak, and that you'll be willing to listen when you're finished speaking.

Avoid staring aggressively or engaging in hostile glares. And avoid looking up, down, and around the person to whom you're speaking. Such evasive eye contact conveys uncertainty and anxiety.

Be Aware of Your Body Orientation

Your physical position in relation to the people with whom you're speaking is called body orientation. Your body orientation should be similar to that of the people you're addressing: If they're seated, you should be seated; if they're standing, you should stand.

Respect their personal space by not standing too close and not physically trapping them against a wall or in a corner. For example, standing very close to a person to whom you're expressing anger could be interpreted as aggressive, threatening, or hostile. You want the other person to feel comfortable, not threatened or trapped, whether your message is appropriately positive or necessarily negative. People who feel threatened or trapped don't listen well and usually don't remember the words; they only remember the sense of being in danger.

Pay Attention to the Quality of Your Voice

Deliver your assertive messages in a voice that's firm, warm, and expressive. Speak loudly enough to be heard, increasing your volume slightly from time to time for emphasis.

Avoid a high-pitched, whiny tone. If you suspect your tone is high-pitched or nasal, check to see whether you're smiling as you speak. People who usually smile when they speak tend to have a high-pitched, nasal, somewhat whiny voice quality. Drop the smile, and it will lower the pitch of your voice.

Pace your speech so that you speak neither too rapidly nor too slowly. Check with your listener from time to time to make sure you aren't moving too quickly from idea to idea; belaboring points, and thus moving too slowly from idea to idea; repeating yourself; or speaking with a disturbing hesitation. Vocal quality that's pleasant to the ear and confident in delivery enhances and emphasizes the assertive content of your message.

Listen

Finally, when you're being assertive, take time to listen. After you've made an assertion, listening will help you check to see that the other person has clearly understood what you have said. For example, you might stop speaking for a time and ask, "Does this make sense to you?" or a similar question that would give you a chance to hear the other person's ideas about what you've said. You might discover early in the conversation that your listener is too excited or fearful to take in everything you'd planned to say. You can then make a midcourse correction and concentrate on just a few points delivered in an especially nonthreatening way.

Careful listening also contributes to effective, assertive communication because listening shows respect for the other person. Listening is part of the overall assertive message you want to deliver, which includes not only what you say and how you say it, but also how carefully and respectfully you listen to the other person's response.

Assertive communication integrates words, actions, style, and substance into an effective message that accurately communicates what you want to say. Assertive communication includes listening, both because it helps you realize whether your message is getting through and because it marks the respect you always maintain for the other. With assertive communication, the whole is greater than the sum of its parts.

PART FOUR

Opportunities for Assertiveness

10

How to Make Requests

Collyer struggled down the aisle of the airplane clutching the boarding passes in one hand, trying to balance Jeremy in his safety seat as he leaned heavily to the left in order to keep the diaper bag securely on his right shoulder.

Bumping some passengers and nudging others, he murmured, "Excuse me," "Sorry, ma'm," "Excuse me, sir."

Collyer and Jeremy were joining flight 782 at its second stop, and most of the other passengers had been comfortably settled since the flight took off from Pensacola an hour ago.

"Eighteen, nineteen, twenty," he counted the rows. "Only three more." Row 23, seats B and C, aisle and middle. The aisle seat for Collyer and his long legs, and the middle seat for Jeremy in his safety seat.

What a relief it will be to sit down was all he could think.

Imagine Collyer's surprise to find a businessman comfortably settled in row 23, seat C. Collyer glanced quickly at the boarding passes still crunched in his hand, and checked the row and seat designation above the seats.

The businessman looked up from the work he had spread out on the tray table. Collyer said, "Excuse me, but I'm assigned this seat, and my son has the seat next to you."

The man looked directly at Collyer and responded, "Could you sit in the window seat?"

Collyer had been patient all morning. He had managed to drive to the airport, park the car, carry Jeremy and all that equipment down the long concourses, wait at the gate, struggle down the aisle—and now this. He lost his composure and his temper.

"You're in my seat and I want my seat. I reserved an aisle seat and I want an aisle seat. You've no right to be there, and you've no right to ask me to sit at the window. I want my seat, and I want it now!"

Collyer's anger and impatience are in a way understandable, given his stressful situation. But his instinctively aggressive expression of exasperation and impatience will probably only increase his stress level and is no guarantee that he'll solve his primary problem with the airplane seats. Collyer needs to ask for what he wants and he needs to ask assertively, so that his request is simple, direct, and effective.

Sharon and Gordon Bower describe a technique for assertively making requests that they call DESC Scripts. According to the Bowers, an assertive request should have all four components.

Describe the Situation (D)

Tell how the situation appears to you in behavioral terms. Describe what you see, hear, or experience as objectively as if it were recorded on a camera or tape recorder. For example:

• "This floral arrangement was delivered to my home this afternoon. Because no one was home at the time, the flowers were left on the porch. The cold has seriously damaged the flowers."

• "Two weeks ago you came to my door and asked if you could take a shortcut through our yard to the next street on your way to school. I agreed, as long as you promised to close the gate carefully every time so that our dog wouldn't get out. For the first week, I noticed that the gate was closed. This week, the gate was left open on Tuesday and Wednesday."

• "When we met six weeks ago, you and I agreed that you'd work to improve your performance in two important areas: arriving at work on time each morning and eliminating all but the most necessary personal telephone calls during working hours. The records indicate that in six weeks you've been late to work once, and that was the day of the ice storm. I've noticed that you spend significantly less time on personal telephone calls now. These are important and positive changes."

Express Your Feelings about the Situation (E)

This is a good time to use I messages. Speak personally about what feelings, if any, the situation has aroused in you. Own the feelings as your own, use I messages, and avoid statements that imply the other person makes you feel the way you do. For example:

• "I'm very disappointed that the flowers are no longer attractive and useful."

• "I'm worried that some day our dog will run away because the gate has been left open."

• "I'm pleased that you've been able to make such significant changes in your personal work habits."

Specify What You Want (S)

Surprisingly, this is the step most people miss when they want to make a request! Ask for what you want, and ask specifically. This is a good time to use I want statements. Make your requests manageable and reasonable, and make only one or two requests at a time. For example:

• "I'd like to have the flowers replaced and delivered before seven o'clock, in time for our party tonight."

• "I want you to close the gate each time you come through our yard."

• "I'd like you to continue to be on time each day and keep personal phone calls to a minimum, as you've been doing."

Describe the Consequences Associated with Your Request (C)

Whenever possible, describe the positive consequences associated with your request. Threats and predictions of dire consequences often awaken defensiveness and anger in listeners, and their attention shifts to defensive or hostile behavior. If you want cooperation, show them how cooperating with your request will be in their best interest as well as yours. If you must specify negative consequences, make sure the consequence is appropriate, and choose only consequences that you're willing to carry out. For example:

• "Fresh flowers would really make the anniversary party we're giving a special occasion. I'd be very grateful if you would make the effort to have the flowers replaced in time for the party."

• "I'm happy to have you cut through the yard because I know it saves you time. If you continue to leave the gate open, however, you may not use the shortcut through our yard anymore."

• "You've asked about a promotion. If you can maintain those good work habits of being on time and keeping personal phone calls to a minimum until the next performance review in six weeks, I'll be happy to talk to you about the position of departmental assistant at that time."

Following the DESC Scripts above doesn't guarantee that you'll get what you request. Your request may open the door to further conversation and negotiation with the other person, your request may be denied, or you may have to wait for your request to be granted at some future time. Making requests assertively—clearly, concisely, and directly—does ensure that both you and the other person know just what you want, why you want it, and what the significance of that request is for both of you. Such straightforward communication is genuinely assertive.

11

Granting, Refusing, or Negotiating Requests

A wonderful Jewish story is told about a Teacher and one of his companions who called on a rich man to seek funds for a man who had suffered a severe heart attack.

The host greeted the Teacher and his friend warmly and listened intently as the Teacher briefly described the desperate plight of the one who had suffered the ailment. "We are asking you for a generous gift," the Teacher concluded.

"Who is the sick man?" the host asked.

The Teacher shook his head. "Rarely do we reveal the names of people in need. In this case, it is most difficult for the man to admit that he needs charity."

"If I am to help, I insist on knowing the identity of the man in need. I will keep it in strictest confidence. I was going to give you $500, but if you tell me the man's name, I will increase the gift to $1,000."

"We will not reveal the man's name," the Teacher said, shaking his head.

"Two thousand dollars. Surely you will not refuse such an amount."

"I will not break confidence," the Teacher insisted. His friend looked at him in disbelief.

Taking a deep breath, the host said, "Three thousand dollars."

Before the Teacher could reply, his companion pleaded with him. "Teacher, three thousand dollars will pay for all the hospital and living expenses. He is an honorable man; he can keep the secret with us."

The Teacher walked toward the door. "I should have left long ago. The honor of a man is not open to barter or negotiation regardless of what the sum of money might be. I have other visits to make."

Before the Teacher could leave the house, the rich man begged him to meet with him privately in the next room. The moment they were alone, the rich man broke into tears. "Teacher, I recently lost every penny I saved. I am not able to make even a token payment on the mortgage. I have wanted to go to someone for help, but I couldn't stand the idea of everyone in the city knowing that I am a failure."

"Now I understand," the Teacher said tenderly. "You were testing me to see if I could be trusted with your secret. I will seek funds for you as well as for the man who is sick. What you have told me will be kept in confidence."

People are often inclined to grant the requests others make of them whether they are reasonable requests or not. Sometimes people simply want others to like them, sometimes they're eager to make others happy, and sometimes it's just easier to grant rather than refuse a request.

As the Teacher's story so aptly illustrates, however, sometimes an individual must refuse another's request. In this instance, the Teacher was concerned about keeping confidential the identity of the person who was ill. In the same way, you may want to refuse to divulge information about a sister's divorce, the cost of a new car, or the details of a recent surgery. At times personal judgment or preference prompts people to refuse a request.

In Matthew 5:37 (NIV), Jesus encourages you to be honest when confronted with an opportunity to say yes or no. "'Simply let your "Yes" be "Yes," and your "No," "No"; anything beyond this comes from the evil one.'" When you know your answer to a request, you are to give that yes or no straightforwardly. Jesus also warns that to equivocate when you know what you should be doing opens the door to temptation. People may be tempted to lie to keep friends. They may violate their personal integrity as they intentionally give a mistaken impression. They may delay the Lord's work or harm the well-being of another while they take unreasonable amounts of time to announce a decision. Or they may frustrate other people and harm their relationships by repeatedly changing from yes to no and back again. What wisdom the Lord shares! "'Simply let your "Yes" be "Yes," and your "No," "No."'"

Responding to requests is based primarily on two rights: the right others have to make a request, and the right you have to grant, refuse, or negotiate another's request. Along with these two rights goes your right to have all the information you need to be fully aware of the nature of the request. If you don't fully understand a request, you may later regret your decision, whether your answer is no or yes.

If you need some time to consider a decision, you also have the right to postpone your decision. Don't use postponement as a means to avoid saying no or yes to a request, however. That would be manipulative, and assertiveness doesn't involve even a small amount of manipulation.

During the period of indecision that may naturally precede a decision, assertive principles apply: Show respect for the other person while respecting your own needs, preferences, and limitations. That means you try to be as sensitive as possible to the person who is making the request while you avoid being rushed or pushed into a decision. Consider the following example:

Joe: "Our second grade Sunday school teacher abruptly quit after class last Sunday, and we need a new teacher right away. Will you be the new second grade Sunday school teacher, at least for the next six months, until the end of the school year?"

Kim: "I can see that you're in a very difficult spot, Joe, and that you need to fill that position before next Sunday. Your request is coming as quite a surprise to me, though, and I need some time to think about it before I make a decision. I also want to see the teaching materials used for the second grade level."

Joe: "I sure hope you can do it. I'm in a real fix, since the second grade is one of our largest classes. If you say no, I don't know whom I'll ask."

Kim: "I enjoy teaching children, and I've taught Sunday school before. I need to decide if I have enough time to prepare the lessons each week. And I need to decide if I can give up the adult class I've been attending. Could you gather the teaching materials so that I could look at what has been taught and get an idea of the curriculum for the rest of the year? Maybe we could meet Tuesday evening and discuss your offer. By that time, I can get my thoughts together and have some questions for you. I think I can have a decision by the end of our meeting on Tuesday so that, if I'm not able to do it, you'd still have time to ask someone else."

Joe: "That sounds fair to me. How about 7:30 Tuesday evening, in the second grade classroom?"

Notice that in this example:

1. Kim expressed sensitivity to Joe's predicament.

2. Both parties shared feelings, I messages, and I want statements.

3. Kim was not swayed to make a hasty decision by the urgency of the situation.

4. Both parties agreed on a time by which the decision would be made.

5. Both parties made specific requests.

This is an example of an assertive exchange because the needs and preferences of both parties were respected and considered as part of the decision-making process.

Granting Requests

If you have trouble saying no, you may also have trouble saying yes when you really want to do so. If you almost always feel compelled to grant requests, you're rarely in a position to decide to say yes when you want to do so. Your decision-making process depends on others and the requests they make, not on you. Thus, you're rarely in a position to say yes freely, because of a genuine desire to do something. Your yes will be passive rather than assertive. Your commitment will probably be halfhearted, and you probably won't feel very satisfied about your involvement with the request.

It's just as important to say an assertive yes as it is to say an assertive no. When you assertively say yes to a request, you're not just passively going along with it, for an assertive yes includes commitment. It signals your willingness to invest effort. It tells the other person you'll be glad to do it. Assertively saying yes gives others your full support and gives you the opportunity to enjoy what is requested of you. To be true to yourself and to properly honor the requests of others, you need to be able to say an assertive yes as well as an assertive no.

Sometimes You Grant a Request with Enthusiasm

When assertively granting a request, it's possible to enhance the relationship with the person making the request. You can accomplish this by choosing your words thoughtfully, by using I messages, and by paying careful attention to the other person. For example, your yes can affirm the friendship:

Request: "Do you have time to go shopping with me on Saturday morning? I know you've been extra busy lately, but I'd really like your help in selecting a dress for the party."

Response: "I'd be delighted to go shopping with you on Saturday. One of the hard parts about my busy schedule is that I haven't been able to spend as much time with you as I'd like. I miss you, and I'll look forward to shopping together on Saturday morning."

Saying yes to this request became an occasion to affirm the other person's value as well as the friendship.

Using I statements when you say yes can also give you the opportunity to share enthusiasm for a project or cause. Although a simple yes is sufficient, you may want to add a supportive statement to certain yeses. For example:

Request: "After eight months of planning, we're going to construct the park's new children's playground on the next two Saturday mornings. Would you be willing to bring your tools to the park at 8:00 A.M. and give us a hand?"

Response: "I've been reading the progress reports about the playground for many months now, and I'd be happy to help. We've needed a safe playground for the neighborhood kids for years, and I really appreciate all the work you folks have put into this project. It will be great to be a part of it, and I'll be there Saturday morning!"

Sometimes You Grant a Request with Reservation

Sometimes you will say yes to a request, but you'll also need to let the other person know that you have some hesitancy about part of the request. If the reservation you have is not strong enough to generate a no response nor central enough to invite a negotiated response, you might honestly and assertively say yes while expressing the reservations. For example,

Request: "I have a few errands to run this afternoon, and my car is being repaired again. Could I use your car?"

Response: "I'm reluctant to lend you my car because the last two times you used it you returned it late. Both times I ended up having to postpone what I needed to do. I'll agree to lend you my car this time, but I expect you to return it on time. Let's agree that, if you return it late this time, you may not borrow it again."

Refusing Requests

For many people, saying no to a request is very difficult. People may believe that they don't have the right to refuse a request, especially a friend's request; people may fear that if they say no, others will become angry; some people may believe that if they say no, they'll hurt the other's feelings.

But because they're unable to say no to requests, people often become involved in activities they later regret. They may find themselves unfairly used, abused, or manipulated into doing things they don't want to do. People who habitually fail to say no to requests can become suspicious of their relationships with others, and they tend to feel defensive and resentful when others make requests.

Here are some guidelines for assertively refusing a request.

When Possible, Let People Know in Advance That You Will Say No

Giving advance warning prepares the person for your eventual action, gives you the opportunity to reduce the anxiety involved in the situation, and tends to discourage people from asking you for the favor or request. Advance warning also decreases the hope that other people have of getting what they want, so they may be less persistent.

Say No Simply and Politely

Avoid overtalking, long drawn-out sentences, and convoluted reasoning. A simple, straightforward, assertive refusal sends the message that you mean what you say. Avoid trying to soften the no with qualifiers and explanations. Here is a request with several possible responses:

Request: "Hey, Janie, a bunch of us are going out to the base-ball game this afternoon. Want to come?"

Response (passive): "Gosh, I really wish I could go but I've just got gobs and gobs of work to do. Yesterday my boss gave me a sixteen-page report to have done by Tuesday, and the kids have soccer games and cheerleading practice. Bob's out of town or I would see if I could get him to take Timmy to soccer, but then I'd still have the report to do for work. I just don't see how I can go, and I hope you guys aren't mad."

Response (aggressive): "Well, some of us have to work, you know. You guys are always goofing off. Didn't you go to the game last week, too? Do you ever get any work done?"

Response (assertive): "Thanks for inviting me, but this is really a busy week. I hope I can go with you next time."

Give a Reason or Explanation Only If You Choose to Do So

Offering an explanation for your refusal is your choice, not an obligation. You can be assertive in choosing whether or not to give a reason for your no.

You may want to avoid giving a reason for your refusal if you believe that the person may use your statement to argue with you or to try to talk you out of your decision.

If a friend or someone with whom you share a close per-sonal relationship makes a request that you decide to refuse, however, you'll probably want to give an explanation—not out of guilt or fear of rejection or anger, but because giving an explanation will keep healthy communication and posi-tive feelings between you. Your refusal and brief explanation could provide an opportunity to deepen your mutual under-standing and help nurture your good relationship.

Avoid Starting with an Apology

You have a right to refuse a request, and you don't have to apologize. But if you're genuinely sorry to have to refuse the request and you want the other person to know it, by all means say so. Avoid overstating how sorry you are or apologizing too extensively because your apologies will decidedly weaken the firmness of your no. It may also occur to the person that if you dislike saying no so much, you might as well say yes and save yourself all the misery.

Repeat Your Message Firmly and Kindly Until the Other Person Hears Your Refusal

An assertive refusal respects both the person making the request and the person who decides to refuse the request. For example, at a friend's birthday party you meet a person who sells soil-testing kits. He tells you about environmental dangers and urges you to buy several kits to periodically test the soil in your backyard. You're not interested in purchasing this product; when you refuse, he persists.

Request: "You're really making a mistake. Instead of six kits, how about three?"

Response: "No, thanks. I'm not interested in buying any kits."

Request: "You owe it to your family to test the soil regularly. Do you want your kids to get sick?"

Response: "I'm not interested in buying any kits."

Request: "I'll tell you what. If you buy three kits, I'll throw in a fourth kit for free. How about it?"

Response: "Thanks, but I don't want to buy any kits."

Request: "Well, okay. I guess I can't sell you any kits today. Here's my card in case you change your mind."

Pay Attention to Your Nonverbal Messages

Your nonverbal messages sent through voice, gestures, eye contact, and posture must be consistent with the refusal you speak or you'll confuse your listener. A firm, assertive refusal requires straightforward eye contact, clear delivery of the message, and erect posture. The message you want to convey is that you do mean what you're saying.

Avoid Equating Refusal of a Request with Rejection of the Person or the Relationship

If you refuse a person's request, you aren't rejecting the person or the relationship. Henry Close makes this point in "On Saying No to People: A Pastoral Letter":

> When I say NO to people, I am saying NO to *one aspect* of a relationship. I am not saying NO to the whole relationship. But many people don't understand this. They take any NO as a complete rejection of them, and feel terribly hurt and rejected. They may use this feeling of rejection as a means of bribery or blackmail. "If you won't do such and such for me, I guess there's just nothing left for me to live for," or, "If you won't come with us, then none of us will go." To withstand this kind of pressure (blackmail), I need to understand clearly that my NO's are to *one* aspect of the relationship, not the whole thing, no matter how offended the other person acts.[1]

Don't Try to Talk the Other Person out of the Request

Sometimes it's so hard to refuse a request that people try to avoid dealing with the request. One such sidestepping

---

1 Henry Close, "On Saying No to People: A Pastoral Letter," *Journal of Pastoral Care* 28:2 (1974), p. 95.

technique is to try to talk the other person out of making the request. "You don't really mean that," "How could you ask that?" and "Are you kidding?" all attempt to get the other to withdraw the request so one won't have to refuse it.

Respect for the other means that you take his or her requests seriously and assume that each request is sincerely made. Discounting or minimizing the request is usually aggressive.

Learn to Graciously, Assertively Allow Others to Say No to You

Because assertive interactions are respectful of both parties, learn to accept a no from another person without getting angry, feeling rejected, arguing, or trying to change the person's mind. You may use I messages to express your feelings about the refusal, but inflicting guilt, manipulating, and responding disrespectfully are aggressive behaviors. For example, you have two tickets to the community theater production of *Our Town*. You know your best friend, Marge, loves the play as much as you do, so you ask her to go with you. She declines, saying that she promised to teach her grandchildren how to make pretzels that night, and the children have been looking forward to it for weeks.

Response (passive): "Well, okay, if you don't want to go with me, that's okay, I guess. I just hate to go to plays alone."

Response (aggressive): "Come on, Marge! You love *Our Town*. Just change the pretzel-making to another night. Who knows when we'll get to see this play again!"

Response (assertive): "I'm sorry you can't go with me, and I can understand that you're looking forward to spending that evening with your grandchildren. We'll plan another time to get together."

Negotiating Requests

In some circumstances an immediate and clear yes or no isn't possible. You may need to propose changes that would make you more inclined to grant the request or clarify issues that will help you decide whether to grant or refuse the request.

To *negotiate* means "to discuss"; the nature of negotiation is dialogue. The person making the request and the person who initiates the negotiation enter into a process of discussion and dialogue, listening carefully to each other and trying to reach a mutually acceptable outcome. For example, you are home alone and have planned a busy afternoon of reading, working, and catching up on tasks that you've been putting off. Your next-door neighbor calls and asks if you'll babysit with her three-year-old for two or three hours until her mother-in-law arrives. The friend says that she's been called in to work at two and can find no other child care. You'd be glad to take care of the child for two hours, but no more than that. You might start a negotiation by saying:

You: "I'd be happy to care for Sean for two hours, but no more. I have some very important things to do today. Who will care for him after four?"

She: "Well, actually, it might end up being three or four hours before Bill's mom can get here. But my other neighbor said he could take care of Sean later in the afternoon. I'll call and see if he could take Sean at four."

You: "That's fine. If he'll take Sean at four, I'll be glad to take care of him from two until four. At four I'll see that he gets to your neighbor's house. Will you call me back and let me know if your neighbor will take Sean at four?"

Such negotiation allows both parties the opportunity to discuss their needs and to talk about how they can cooperate to get those needs met. Assertive negotiation involves mutual respect and is a sign that you care for others, even as you honor your own limitations.

In the example above, the mother asked for what she needed; you responded with a statement of your willingness to help within your time limitations. She proposed a possible solution. You agreed to her proposal and asked for a confirming phone call when arrangements were in place. Both parties were honest about needs and limitations and both parties were willing to help the other get those needs met.

Here are some guidelines for negotiating a request.

Be Specific about Which Part of the Request You Want to Negotiate

What is it you really want? Be specific and clear. If you want to negotiate more than one part of a request, discuss only one part at a time.

Avoid Apologizing for Your Limitations or Preferences

You have a right to ask for certain conditions or changes and don't need to apologize for doing so. Remember that asking for certain conditions or changes doesn't obligate the other person to provide them.

Listen Carefully to the Other Person's Request and Possible Counterproposals

What does this person really want? Check out your hunches and ideas by listening carefully and then asking for confirmation of what you think you hear. You might say something like this: "You want me to park in my driveway instead of on the street in front of my house because you're afraid you'll hit my car when you pull out of your driveway. Is that what you're saying?" The person making the request may then correct your impression or agree with your statement, and both of you can then work out an agreement about where the car will be parked.

Continue Negotiating Until You Reach a Mutually Acceptable Outcome or Agree to Cease Negotiations

Be willing to continue negotiations, listening and discussing alternatives, until you reach an outcome acceptable to both parties. For example:

Don't Say: "That's it. That's my first and final offer. Take it or leave it."

Do Say: "I believe we can reach an agreement that will be good for both of us, and I'm willing to keep working at it with you. I think we need to keep talking about this, and I'm willing to do that."

If both parties believe that the goal of negotiation is to reach a mutually acceptable outcome, neither party needs to feel undue pressure for a quick resolution or fear that the other party will prematurely close off negotiations. Simply stating your intent to remain in the negotiations substantially reduces counterproductive pressure and fear.

Over time you may both realize that a mutually agreeable outcome isn't possible, in which case you can agree to stop negotiation.

Whether you want to grant, refuse, or negotiate a request, assertive behaviors will serve you well and protect both you and the person making the request. Of course, just making a request doesn't guarantee that it will be granted. But the use of assertive, respectful responses by one or both parties increases the likelihood that the request will be satisfactorily answered and the relationship enhanced.

12

Offering and Receiving Criticism

An old man and his grandson were traveling from one city to another. At first the boy rode the donkey. But the man heard some people say, "Would you look at that old man suffering on his feet while that strong young boy is totally capable of walking?"

So then the old man rode the donkey while the boy walked. And he heard some people say, "Would you look at that, a healthy man making the poor young boy suffer. Can you believe it?"

So the man and the boy both rode the donkey, and they heard some people say, "Would you look at those heavy brutes making that poor donkey suffer." So they both got off and walked, until they heard some people say, "Would you look at the waste—a perfectly good donkey not being used."

In the final scene, the boy is walking and the old man is carrying the donkey.

No matter what you do, someone can always criticize it.

Criticism is to be expected. Most people have opinions about the lifestyle, behaviors, purchases, plans, choices, and beliefs of others. Humans are a comparing species, and many people have developed the habit of forming an opinion on everything from public policy, community standards, and the behavior of coworkers and neighbors to the choices and decisions of friends and family members. Individuals compare what they have done or think they would do with what others have done and are doing. As in the story, most criticism comes from people's own sense of what they believe is the right thing to do in a given situation.

Deep within every human being is a craving to be right.

People initiate and prolong arguments trying to prove their rightness; they pronounce others wrong who don't follow what they think is right. The need to be right sometimes pushes people into irrational arguments and stinging criticism. Sometimes that need to be right hurts relationships with others.

The good news is that God, because of Jesus' death on the cross, has already declared you righteous! You don't need to let that inner pressure for justification and rightness govern your relationships. You can form an opinion, offer a suggestion, say what you think, express your preferences. But you don't always have to be right.

Sometimes you'll be right; sometimes you won't. Sometimes another's sense of right is as valid as yours. Giving and receiving criticism in a healthy way requires that you acknowledge (particularly to yourself) how much you like to be right—and admit that many issues are actually matters of taste and personal choice.

In the Ten Commandments, God clearly spells out right and wrong behavior. Scripture also clearly defines standards for Christian behavior at work, in families, and in personal lives.

God didn't, however, speak to every issue and circumstance in a Christian's life. God gave people minds to evaluate choices and to make decisions. Often people must prayerfully, carefully make their own choices.

Whether you decide to ride the donkey, walk beside the donkey, or in the end carry the donkey, others may have sincere but conflicting ideas about what is appropriate. But criticism isn't by definition negative. The word *criticism* originally was used to describe evaluation that was as likely to point out positive as negative qualities. Though criticism has taken on a negative connotation in passing years, in the world of fine arts and literature the word *criticism* still retains its balanced meaning, so that a critical review of a Broadway play might well result in "critical acclaim," that is, the praise of critics! In the same way, a critical review of a restaurant in which the restaurant is generously praised is still a critical review.

In its purest sense, therefore, offering criticism only means exercising evaluative judgment about a matter. In this chapter, you'll examine the offering and receiving of criticism that points out the need for improvement or correction. In Chapter 14, you'll deal with how to offer and receive critical evaluations such as compliments and praise.

Offering Criticism

Assertively offering criticism requires that you respect the other's right to make choices while at the same time respecting your own attitudes about an issue. Here are some guidelines for offering criticism assertively.

Carefully Define the Goal of Your Criticism

What do you want to accomplish by offering this criticism? Do you want to ask for a specific behavior change? Do you want the person you're criticizing to think new thoughts, develop new attitudes, or both? Do you want less of some behaviors and more of others?

Decide beforehand what your specific goal is so that you don't get sidetracked by other topics or secondary goals. For example, in expressing displeasure about the condition of your car when your teen returns it:

Don't Say: "The car's a mess! If you can't do better than that, you can't use the car anymore!"

Do Say: "When you return the car, I want you to remove all candy wrappers, cups, and other trash and make sure the interior is as clean as it was when you left. Better yet, use the plastic trash bag we keep in the car."

Note that in the Do Say example, the person not only expressed displeasure about the car's condition but also suggested how to improve the situation.

Get Your Motives Straight

What moves you to offer this criticism—really? One of the most loving things a person can do is to offer loyal criticism—criticism that comes from deep commitment to and genuine concern for the other person. The motivation behind loyal criticism is the welfare of the person you criticize.

You also need to ask yourself, however, if any part of your motivation is to hurt, to get even, or to embarrass the other person. Or have you transformed a personal preference into a "holy cause," using religious language to talk about what is purely personal bias? Often people aren't fully aware of their motives. Spend some time quietly reflecting on your motives for offering criticism.

Just Because You Don't Like It Doesn't Make It Wrong

Many situations have a wide range of acceptable behaviors and most problems have a variety of solutions, all God-pleasing and potentially useful. Beware of translating your personal preferences into terms of right and wrong.

Expect Defensiveness

Most reasonable people don't want to hear things about themselves that imply a need for improvement. And most reasonable people resist change, with all its discomfort and inconvenience. It makes sense, then, that people will defend their positions and resist suggestions for change.

Listen to Reasons, Explanations, Even a Few Excuses

The key word is *listen*. Try to see the situation from the other person's point of view. You don't have to agree or approve, but you can listen for understanding. The careful listener can pick up clues as to what would be a wise approach as the interaction continues.

Invite the other person to respond to your suggestions

for change. Ask, "Is there any reason you think this won't work?" or "Are you willing to give these suggestions a try?" or "What do you think might happen if you implement these changes?"

Four Steps for Offering Criticism

Here are some steps to follow when offering criticism.

1. Describe the situation. Be brief. Be specific. Whenever you can, point to specific behaviors.

2. Use I messages to describe your perceptions and reactions. Speak only for yourself.

3. Offer specific suggestions for improvement. Describe not only what you think is wrong but also suggestions for what you think can be done to make it right.

4. Genuinely assure the person of your help and support before, during, and after the changes are made.

Give the Other Person Time to Recover and Reflect

When hearing a criticism for the first time, most people react defensively, then perhaps angrily. Only after some time has elapsed are individuals likely to consider the validity of the other's observations and suggestions. Often in the privacy of their own minds and the solitude of a separate place, people can accept the criticism and respond productively.

Especially if the criticism is of a highly personal nature, allow the person the courtesy and compassion of some time and privacy to deal with your evaluations and suggestions.

Offering Criticism Doesn't Guarantee That the Other Person Will Change or Will See It Your Way

You can't control another person's behavior. Focus on

your own task: offering criticism assertively, constructively, kindly. The rest is up to the other person.

Receiving Criticism

Assertively receiving criticism challenges you to honor the person who offers the criticism by listening carefully, to honor yourself by careful self-examination, and then to prayerfully consider and make any changes that are indicated. Here are some guidelines for assertively receiving criticism.

Hear the Criticism Accurately

The message you think you are receiving may not be the message that's being sent. It's helpful to stop from time to time and check with the critic to see if you are hearing what is being said. You might say:

"Here is what I think you mean . . . *(state what you have heard)*. Is that accurate?"

Or you could say:

"Let me check this out with you. You are saying . . . *(state what you have heard)*. Is that what you mean?"

Wait for the other person to confirm or deny the accuracy of your perceptions.

It's Normal to Feel Defensive

When someone criticizes you, that person is making evaluative statements about your behavior or attitudes. If those evaluations are negative, he or she will usually ask for changes or imply that you need to figure out some changes on your own. Sometimes, especially if the criticism is not delivered constructively or kindly and is of a personal nature, you may feel demeaned or attacked. It's natural to want to defend yourself against these requests for change.

Admit, at least to yourself, that you're defensive. You can admit, too, that you want to resist the work and inconvenience of change.

And, if you're really honest with yourself, you'll admit to that deep inborn need to be *right*, the craving for righteousness. Denying your defensiveness, your resistance to change, and your need to be right can severely limit your ability to receive and profit from criticism. It is normal to feel defensive.

Assume the Critic Means Well

Your critic may be inaccurate, misdirected, misinformed, or just plain wrong, but it usually takes people a good bit of courage to speak to someone about what they consider a problem. They probably won't criticize perfectly, but just the act of offering criticism often signals a commitment to the relationship. If you can manage it, thank your critic sincerely for the concern and candor.

Refuse Abusive Criticism

Of course, not every critic means well. A few critics offer mean-spirited, unkind, and hurtful criticism. Often this criticism takes the form of an accusation. Assertively refuse to be abused by another person. You might say:

"Name-calling and personal insults are unnecessary. What changes are you suggesting I make?"

[or]

"Just what changes do you want to see as a result of our conversation?"

[or]

"If you want to suggest a change, please do it, but I won't allow you to talk to me in an abusive way."

Each of those replies refuses to accept the subjective personal attack or accusation and instead redirects the criticism toward more objective considerations of behavior change.

When religious leaders accused Jesus of being possessed by Satan, he responded not by launching a personal, emotional defense or counterattack but by redirecting their thinking. Jesus replied rationally to their irrational accusation:

And the teachers of the law who came down from Jerusalem said, "He is possessed by Beelzebub! By the prince of demons he is driving out demons."

So Jesus called them and spoke to them in parables: "How can Satan drive out Satan? If a kingdom is divided against itself, that kingdom cannot stand. If a house is divided against itself, that house cannot stand. And if Satan opposes himself and is divided, he cannot stand; his end has come" (Mark 3:22–26 NIV).

Assertive behavior is loving behavior, and that's why assertive Christians not only refuse to behave abusively toward others but also refuse to let others abuse them. It's not a kindness to allow others to abuse you; by allowing abuse, you're actually encouraging sin.

Turn the Spotlight on the Criticism, Not the Critic

One defensive maneuver you may be tempted to try is to discredit the critic by thinking (or saying), "Who does he think he is?" or "Look at the pot calling the kettle black!" or "Who appointed her judge and jury?" Such misdirected attention isn't in your best interest, especially if you can learn from the criticism the person is offering.

Even the most derelict of people may have something useful to offer, and you do yourself and others a disservice when you arbitrarily decide whom you will listen to and whom you will ignore. At the heart of assertiveness is a mutual respect that offers each person a hearing, even if that hearing is brief. While it may be wise in some instances to "consider the source," it's unwise to immediately and arbitrarily reject another person's counsel and criticism.

Learn from Your Critics

Your critics can be your teachers. Criticism thoughtfully conceived and effectively offered is a valuable gift and an affirmation of your value to the critic. No one improves without criticism, and well-meant criticism is an attempt to help another raise his or her level of performance. "Anyone who loves knowledge wants to be told when he is wrong. It is stupid to hate being corrected" (Proverbs 12:1 TEV).

It's Okay to Thoughtfully Reject the Criticism

You may thoughtfully consider criticism and then reject it. You might reply to a friend's criticism that you haven't adequately supported the high school band by saying:

"You know, I've thought a lot about your suggestion that I spend more time promoting the high school band. I can tell you're disappointed that I haven't given as much support as you'd hoped. But my involvement is as much as I want to give at this time. I admire your dedication to the band and thank you for your suggestion."

You can maintain good, strong relationships with people who offer criticism that you choose not to heed. You don't have to refuse the relationship in refusing the criticism.

Admit Sin and Failure

No one is perfect. Sometimes your critic may be right. If so, apologize, acknowledge your shortcomings, and ask for forgiveness.

Others are often God's agents for pointing out sin and failure, and a wise Christian will ask, "What is God saying to me through this?"

Avoid, however, the quick, glib "I'm sorry" or "I was wrong" or "I apologize" if you're simply trying to satisfy or silence the critic. Allow yourself time for reflection so your apology is sincere and leads to appropriate change.

Proverbs 12:15 (TEV) counsels: "Stupid people always think they are right. Wise people listen to advice."

In the End, You Have to Prayerfully Make Up Your Own Mind about Criticism

John Kennedy had a favorite piece of poetry that touched on the often solitary nature of dealing with criticism:

Bullfight critics row on row
Jam the large arena full.
But only one is there who *knows,*
And he's the man who fights the bull.

Is the criticism justified? Do I need to make some changes? What's God telling me through this? Good questions! In the final analysis, even though the opinions of friends and coworkers might give you valuable insight, you are the one who must prayerfully answer those questions and choose a course of action.

Christians who are strong in the Word and persistent in prayer will find themselves more likely to receive criticism in a helpful way. When you must cope with, endure, reflect on, and respond to the criticism of others, you need to use all the resources available to you so that you respond in a way that pleases God and strengthens your relationships.[1]

---

1 To learn more about giving or receiving criticism from a Christian perspective, see *Caring Criticism: Building Bridges Instead of Walls* by William J. Diehm. Available from Stephen Ministries St. Louis (www.stephenministries.org or 314-428-2600).

13

Expressing and Receiving Anger

Once when Leonardo da Vinci was working on his painting "The Last Supper," he became inordinately angry with a certain man. Losing his temper, he lashed the other fellow unfairly with harsh and bitter words. Returning to his canvas, Leonardo attempted to work on the face of Jesus but was so upset he couldn't compose himself for the painstaking work. Finally he put down his tools, sought out the object of his wrath, and asked his forgiveness. The man accepted his apology, and Leonardo could then return to his workshop and finish painting the face of Jesus.

Da Vinci's predicament is a common experience. He became angry, expressed that anger explosively and destructively, then realized to his dismay that he hadn't really settled the matter with the other person or with himself. His creative energy was diverted, his attention distracted; he couldn't work with his whole heart. Only after he apologized for the way he'd expressed his anger could he feel like himself again and get back to work.

Many Christians struggle not only with how to express anger, but also with whether to express anger at all. Well-known Christian writer John Powell says, "When I repress anger, my stomach keeps score." Anger is a most puzzling and mystifying emotion, one that many Christians fear and deny. Many Christians have been taught that anger is a sin, and that seasoned, pious, God-fearing Christians just don't get angry. In a survey of Christian high school students, 65 percent said that healthy Christians don't get angry. One hundred percent of these young Christians also admitted that they feel angry at times!

Anger causes a lot of apprehension and guilt. People sincerely want to please God in their lives and relationships but become confused at times about when to turn the other cheek and when to speak up and hold their ground. Jesus gave many examples of straightforward, assertive confrontations, not only with the Pharisees but also with his disciples and others he loved. But Christians genuinely fear that they'll lose control and sin in expressing their anger.

Instead of facing anger head-on, many find ways to express anger that seem good at the time but that don't encourage healthy relationships and only deepen confusion and guilt.

For example, some people so fear the expression of anger that they deny and hide angry feelings—only to find that the anger seeps out in sarcastic remarks or hurtful jokes and teasing. Television situation comedies that portray family life often use sarcastic, aggressive attempts at humor that demean and humiliate family members. These apparently harmless comments reveal thinly veiled anger and hostility. Snide remarks about a person's physical appearance or caustic references to someone's failure to do household chores are common. In these television comedies, children make sarcastic, disrespectful remarks to parents, and parents provoke their children and make fun of a child's immaturity—all under the guise of humor.

Other people blow up like volcanoes, raining down the white-hot lava of harmful words and accusations. While the angry person may feel better immediately after a blow-up, people with explosive tempers frequently feel guilt and remorse for what they've said and how they said it. And often people who live and work with someone with an explosive temper feel fearful and insecure around that person, never knowing what will set him or her off; the white-hot lava of ugly words has surprised and burned them more than once.

As scary as explosive anger is, another way of expressing anger is equally frightening: Some anger *implodes*. Some anger explodes inward, resulting in depression, a tendency toward addictions, suicidal thoughts, or even suicide. What people hide and deny will dominate them.

Sometimes the anger we refuse to own in one arena erupts in another. A person mad at the boss may come home and kick the dog, discipline the kids too harshly, or yell at other family members.

And for those who simply, by an act of will, refuse to acknowledge anger, physical illness and tension abound. Language declares what an individual might wish to hide: A person is "a pain in the neck"; a situation is "a real headache." People's bodies send signals that reveal repressed, hidden anger. Unacknowledged anger is still inside; your body tells the truth.

Expressing Anger

Expressing anger without resorting to passive or aggressive behavior is difficult. With effort, you can improve your ability to handle angry feelings assertively. Unfortunately, many have been taught the gospel according to Thumper, the rabbit in *Bambi*: "If you can't say anything nice about [or to] someone, don't say anything at all." You can express anger appropriately, however. Wrong comes not in the anger but in the way you express that anger, as Ephesians 4:26 (TEV) admonishes: "If you become angry, do not let your anger lead you into sin, and do not stay angry all day."

Sometimes people believe that if they express anger, others will become upset and relationships will fall apart. Yet hiding angry feelings and stewing over them will probably hurt relationships anyway.

In spite of attempts to keep angry feelings inside, chances are good that they'll leak out in destructive ways such as avoiding others, silence, curtness, sulking, pouting, impatience, blowing up over little incidents, or revenge. Often relationships are broken because one or both people keep anger inside rather than express it.

You can express angry feelings constructively by responding assertively to the situations and the people who are the focus of your anger. By behaving assertively you show care not only for yourself but also for others. Expressing anger assertively lets you get those feelings out of your system and lets others know how you feel so that changes can be made. In most instances, assertive behavior reduces tension so that problems can be solved in a peaceful, healthy manner.

Here are some guidelines for assertively expressing anger.

Own Your Anger

Admitting that you sometimes feel angry is an honest, straightforward act. Admitting that the anger you feel is your own and pledging that you will express anger only in respectful, responsible, assertive ways is to behave in a proactive rather than reactive manner.

Substitute "It Would Be Nice If" for "Should"

Thinking patterns directly influence a person's experiences and expressions of anger. If you frequently think and talk about what others should be doing, you are using your own personal standard for others' behavior. When others don't measure up, you feel angry and disappointed. Most of the time, others don't play by your rules.

Suppose your child has entered first grade at the local elementary school, and you attend the fall PTA meeting, hoping to meet new friends. To your disappointment, a great many of the members already know each other and spend the social time sharing stories of vacations and planning carpools and get-togethers. Afterward, you complain—to yourself and anyone else you encounter.

Don't Say (to yourself or anyone else): "All PTA members should be friendly and welcome newcomers to meetings."

Do Say (to yourself, plus anyone you decide to tell): "It would be nice if all PTA members were friendly and welcomed newcomers to their meetings. I was disappointed that they didn't welcome me."

Sometimes eliminating the *should* from your thinking and speaking may lead you to discover a very different feeling hiding under your anger—in this case, disappointment. Eliminating *should* can also lift some pressure from you; when you use *should,* you often take on the responsibility of controlling the situation so that you can make it right.

Channel Your Anger Energies

Anger is known as the energy emotion. The physiological reaction to anger readies an individual for flight or fight, and you can use the excitement and adrenaline behind anger to make important changes. Mothers Against Drunk Driving (MADD) is a powerful example of individuals who have used their anger about the death or injury of their children to change an entire nation's awareness of and response to drunk driving.

The angry, lonely, disappointed parent who felt ignored at the PTA meeting might channel some of that anger energy into serving on a special PTA committee that would find ways to welcome newcomers to the PTA meetings. Or the parent could find other newcomers, and they themselves could schedule some social time to get to know one another and welcome other newcomers.

Be Concise and Stick to the Issue

Don't harangue and carry on at length about your complaint. Identify what you want to talk about, decide what you want to say, and then say it as briefly, concisely, and firmly as possible. Talk about just one issue at a time.

For example, you have a good relationship with a friend whose company you've enjoyed very much over the years.

Lately, however, your friend is constantly kidding you about your weight. You can take some teasing in stride, but your friend's teasing is no longer enjoyable and, in fact, you're becoming very annoyed. Your friend has just made another joke about your extra pounds.

Don't Say: "You know, Connie, I've been trying really hard to lose some weight, but you never notice that kind of thing, do you? You just think it's real funny to keep at me about my weight! Well, you can just stop now! I don't think you have any right to even comment on my weight. You should look in the mirror first!"

Do Say: "I've been getting very annoyed lately by your frequent joking about my weight. I prefer that you not joke about this any more."

The Don't Say example is aggressive and wordy and only indirectly asks the person to stop the teasing. The Do Say example directly and respectfully asks the person to stop the teasing.

Use "I" Messages and "I Want" Statements

After you decide what behavior you'd like to see changed, speak for yourself. Use the word *I* and avoid quoting other people or other groups who share your opinion. Speak only about your own thoughts and feelings. Ask for specific behavior changes in clear, direct language. Don't use go-betweens to carry your messages, and be honest with the other person about what you think, how you feel, and what you'd like to see changed.

Avoid Labeling, Name-Calling, and Sarcasm

Aggressive behaviors like name-calling and sarcasm only escalate your own anger and encourage defensiveness and anger in others. For example:

Don't Say: "Look who's talking, pudgy! You're not exactly

skinny yourself, you know. Maybe you need to find a weight loss support group."

Do Say: "I don't think your jokes about my weight are funny anymore. I want you to stop joking about my weight."

Stay in the Here and Now

When assertively expressing anger, avoid dragging into the discussion past mistakes, negative personal history, or earlier problems. Focus on the issue at hand and your thoughts and feelings about that issue. If other issues keep popping up, set another time to discuss those issues.

For example, you're the parent of two small children. You see your in-laws frequently and enjoy their company. You're annoyed, however, that they often discipline your children in your own home, in your presence, in ways you don't approve of. You've repeatedly asked them not to do this since you and your spouse want to be the ones to handle disciplining. Your in-laws have just corrected your children for the second time since supper.

Response (passive): Think to yourself that you shouldn't get angry over such things, or silently vow to invite them over as little as possible in the future.

Response (aggressive): "You're both doing exactly the same thing with Bob and Aggie's kids, and they hate it, too! If you keep this up, all your kids and grandkids too are going to hate to see you coming!"

Response (assertive): "Listen to me closely. I've asked you before not to discipline my children in our home. I'm getting very angry that you insist on doing this. We will do the disciplining when we see that it's necessary."

Give the Other Person a Chance to Respond, and Listen Carefully to That Response

It's possible that your anger is based on erroneous information or a mistaken perception. Listen with an open mind to what the other person has to say, respecting that point of view even if you don't agree with it.

For example, your in-laws respond to your assertive response about disciplining your children by saying, "We've raised five children, and all of them have turned out to be fine adults. You should listen to some of our advice. We're only trying to help."

Response (passive): "Yeah, I guess you're right."

Response (aggressive): "Who says your kids turned out fine?"

Response (assertive): "I appreciate your concern. But these are our children and we alone will discipline them in our house. If you want to talk about this after the children go to bed, I'll be glad to listen."

Pray about Your Anger—Hot Metal Can Be Molded

Don't ask God to take away your anger, even though it might be more comfortable. Ask God to reveal to you the hidden feelings behind your anger. Ask God to protect you from overresponding with aggressive behaviors or under-responding with passive, ineffective behaviors. God can give you the courage and judgment to respond in a way that respects yourself as well as others.

Receiving Anger

Being on the receiving end of anger is difficult at best. At worst, it can be a frightening experience, filled with personal danger and threatening behavior. If you're the target of the anger, you might feel uncomfortable, fearful, or confused. You may ask, "What is this all about? What did I do to cause this? How can I make the other person feel better?"

Most people have trouble dealing with others' anger. Even experienced professional counselors find this to be one of the most difficult aspects of clinical practice. It's no wonder, then, that dealing with the anger of your own family members, friends, coworkers, and neighbors is difficult.

Here are some guidelines for assertively receiving another's anger.

Refuse Abuse and Violence

Assertive behavior embraces respect for yourself as well as respect for others. Don't allow yourself to be physically, verbally, or emotionally abused by angry people. Setting limits on the abusive expression of anger protects not only you but the angry person as well. Many people are deeply sorry, embarrassed, and ashamed of their angry words and behavior, and you can help them regain self-control by refusing to accept abusive behavior. You can express those limits assertively and directly. For example:

Don't Say: "Who do you think you are to talk to me that way? Your threats don't scare me! You just think you'll get your way by acting tough!"

Do Say: "You may not talk to me that way. I know you're very angry, but name-calling is going too far. Please stop."

Realize That You May Not Be the Real Target

It's possible that the angry person only finds you readily available, that you're not actually the target of the anger. The office worker who had a disagreement with his boss might decide not to risk his job by responding angrily at work, so when he stops at the dry cleaner's on the way home he angrily complains about the service, the quality of the cleaning, and the cost of cleaning a suit.

Sometimes you may hear lengthy, angry tirades about an injustice, real or imagined. Often you can do two useful things: Listen carefully, then suggest that the person speak directly to the person or persons with whom he or she is angry. Offer to help the person make a simple plan to share anger assertively. Anger isn't well resolved unless it's shared with the object of the anger. In fact, anger directed at a third party usually intensifies because the anger is experienced anew each time the story is retold.

Matthew 18:15 (NRSV) shares wise advice for anyone who has a complaint and is tempted to talk with someone other than the one with whom he or she has the grievance: "'If another member of the church sins against you, go and point out the fault when the two of you are alone.'" He emphasizes the personal, private, confidential meeting between people who may have anger between them.

If You Are Wrong, Apologize

It's very difficult to hear an angry person out, admit wrongdoing, and assertively apologize. But before you apologize, be sure you hear the other person's full story. A premature apology or request for forgiveness doesn't allow the other person to tell you fully what the offense means to him or her.

In apologizing assertively, maintain eye contact, speak distinctly, and let your nonverbal response to the person's complaint be genuine and honest. Hanging your head, fidgeting with keys, or mumbling an apology are all passive behaviors. You don't have to prove you're sorry by groveling; assertive behavior demonstrates self-respect as well as respect for others.

Apologies can actually be aggressive. For example:

Don't Say: "Okay, okay. I'm wrong. I'm always wrong. And you're always right. And you never make mistakes. Must be nice to be perfect and never make mistakes."

Do Say: "I can see that you're angry because we're often late to church, and being late makes you nervous. And I admit that I do linger too long over the Sunday morning paper. I'm sorry, and I want you to know that I'll be ready to leave on time in the future."

The Don't Say example is aggressive in its sarcasm and exaggeration and won't contribute to solving the problem. In all likelihood, it will only invite the angry person to become more angry. The Do Say example assertively acknowledges and respects the angry person's feelings and offers a straightforward apology as well as a commitment to make an important behavior change.

Realize That Some People Are Angry with God

Is it a terrible sin to be angry with God? Not at all. God is hardly the weak, defenseless type who falls apart at a few harsh words. Many of the psalms are filled with anger directed at God—for apparently deserting the psalmist, for allowing the wicked to prosper and at the same time allowing faithful servants to suffer.

God is the only one who is big enough, strong enough, and loving enough to deal with the full range of human feelings, including anger. We are limited in this respect; God is unlimited.

You can follow three steps when someone expresses anger about God to you.

1. Listen carefully. Try to hear the feelings as well as the words. Let the person know what you're hearing.

2. Assure the person that it's not a sin to be angry with God. It's how that anger is expressed that can lead people into sin.

3. Encourage the person to speak directly to God about the anger and the reasons for it, perhaps using one of the "angry psalms" as a prayer. You might suggest

Psalms 10, 22, 38, 74, or 79. A translation in contemporary language or a paraphrase might be especially useful.

Demonstrate Christian Servanthood

Allowing others to express their anger to you, whether they're angry with you or with others, shows true servanthood. You have the opportunity to effect change and healing when you assertively receive another's anger.

Assertively receiving anger means that you respect the other person's anger enough to hear it and honor its meaning for that person. Your initial privilege is simply to receive the anger, not to try to fix it, talk the person out of it, minimize the anger, or make the person feel better.

Sometimes, just by receiving another's anger you help that person deal with it, release it, or decide what to do with it. More often, simply sharing anger with someone else doesn't bring release or healing. You may need to be assertive and help the person identify the anger and make plans that will lead to healing and release.

Dealing effectively with anger demands assertiveness. Many opportunities for sin surround anger; assertive behavior helps you avoid sin and move toward healthy relationships with other people by honestly, assertively dealing with complaints and problems. Anger isn't itself a sin; assertive, proactive choices can help you avoid sin.

14

Offering and Receiving Compliments and Appreciation

A young schoolboy was trying out for a part in the school play. His mother knew that he had set his heart on it, though she was afraid he wouldn't be chosen. On the day the parts were awarded, she drove to school to pick him up. The young lad rushed up to her, eyes shining with pride and excitement. What he said to her contains a lesson for everyone: "I have been chosen to clap and cheer!"

The young boy was given an important part in the school play—and apparently his wise teacher had helped him realize the importance of his part. How valuable the appreciative audience! How encouraging is the sincere compliment, how supportive is the kind word, how heartening is the friendly pat on the back.

Offering Compliments and Appreciation

Offering compliments, praise, and encouragement is as much a part of the assertive lifestyle as offering suggestions for improvement or expressing anger. Most people enjoy being praised and appreciated even though they may not always know how to receive compliments and appreciation assertively. Praise and appreciation can open the door to healthy relationships with people, and people more readily accept your criticism if you've shared praise and encouragement with them in the past.

Although many people have some idea of what they do well and the talents and skills that they possess, many don't.

For anyone, a word of praise and a sincere compliment may help to affirm what the individual already knows or hopes to be true. A compliment helps an individual understand what personal characteristics are outstanding and unique; a compliment helps an individual learn about him- or herself. And compliments are part of the self-correcting feedback people rely on to assess how they are doing; people repeat behavior that is rewarded and frequently eliminate behavior that is ignored or criticized. The challenge is to maintain a healthy level of self-appraisal and self-awareness so that personal self-esteem and sense of self don't depend entirely on the feedback of others. Remember, whether people are offering praise or censure, they can be wrong.

When you consider the heartening effect of just one compliment sincerely offered, you have to marvel that people are often stingy with such a powerful means of showing appreciation. But many people do hesitate to offer compliments. Sometimes people honestly believe that compliments aren't necessary. People may have trouble offering compliments related to their activities at church, falsely assuming that others don't need to be appreciated or encouraged because their work will be rewarded by God in the end. Some people are especially reluctant to express appreciation to pastors, church staff members, and lay leaders because they're sure that these dedicated people aren't primarily interested in hearing praise for their work. While that may be true, everyone needs to hear an occasional word of gratitude and, from time to time, an acknowledgment of his or her special skills and gifts.

St. Paul knew the value of sincere praise and didn't hesitate to shower praise, appreciation, affection, and encouragement on his Christian brothers and sisters:

> I want to see you more than just briefly in passing; I hope to spend quite a long time with you, if the Lord allows (1 Corinthians 16:7 TEV).

I am so sure of you; I take such pride in you! (2 Corinthians 7:4a TEV).

For this reason, ever since I heard of your faith in the Lord Jesus and your love for all of God's people, I have not stopped giving thanks to God for you. I remember you in my prayers (Ephesians 1:15–16 TEV).

Brother Philemon, every time I pray, I mention you and give thanks to my God. . . . Your love, dear brother, has brought me great joy and much encouragement! You have cheered the hearts of all of God's people (Philemon 4, 7 TEV).

At times you may hesitate to compliment people in authority or high position because you assume that they're praised frequently and well. To be in such a position, they must already know the fine quality of their work and the fact that many people admire them. However, people in public office or in professions that have high visibility often comment that the only kind of feedback they can be sure they'll receive is *negative*. No wonder Mark Twain once said, "I can live on one sincere compliment for several weeks!"

Often people tell others about someone's good qualities but fail to offer the compliment directly to the person they admire. Sometimes compliments die on people's lips because they feel self-conscious, embarrassed, or tongue-tied when they want to express appreciation or admiration; they may decide to take a safer route and not offer the compliment at all. Or a compliment might get caught in people's throats if they're afraid that the person they'd like to praise might brush it off, minimize their offering, or think that the compliment is an attempt to get something from him or her. Such fears often result when someone tried to offer a sincere compliment to another who didn't know how to receive a compliment assertively.

Here are some guidelines for offering appreciation assertively.

Make Your Compliment Brief, Concise, and to the Point

Long-winded, extended speeches may confuse the listener and obscure what you want to say. For example, if you want to compliment the chairperson of a committee:

Don't Say: "You know, I really like all the ideas you have for our committee. You always seem to know just what to do, and that's a big change from the last chairperson, who always had to depend on us for even the most basic information. Some of our meetings were so long and we never even had refreshments. The babysitter always had to stay late and . . ."

Do Say: "I like the way you're leading our committee. We get a lot done at each meeting and I appreciate the fact that you take charge."

The Don't Say example is so drawn out that the compliment is buried beneath all the words and wandering ideas. The Do Say example is straightforward, and it's easy to hear what the compliment is about.

To accept such a compliment assertively, be brief and to the point: "Thank you. I feel good about what we're accomplishing."

Make Your Compliment Specific

Whenever possible, focus your compliment or appreciative statement on a specific behavior, personal quality, or situation. Name what it is you like and appreciate and tell why you like it. A focused compliment is more likely to be remembered.

For example, your friends have just moved into a new home and you are visiting them for the first time. They've spent a great deal of time and energy redecorating, and you can tell that they're justifiably proud of their work.

Don't Say: "Gee, this is really nice. What a nice home."

Do Say: "I like the wallpaper you've chosen. It's really bright and cheerful, and makes the room seem very sunny. And I can see that you put a lot of work into refinishing the floors. They look great!"

Be Spontaneous and Creative

A spontaneous and creative compliment or word of praise is a wonderful gift. The genuineness of the expression is hard to miss when it's delivered in a clear, direct, open, and creative manner. If you're tempted to tell a speaker how much you enjoyed his presentation, take a moment to do so. If you appreciated a soloist's offering of music, tell her. Say what's on your heart in a spontaneous, brief, and sincere outpouring of appreciation.

When Necessary, Affirm Your Original Statement

If someone minimizes or struggles with receiving your compliment or praise, respond with a brief affirmation of your original statement. For example, you compliment the chairperson of the building committee at your church by saying, "That was an excellent report you gave tonight. You must have done a lot of work to prepare it."

She responds passively with, "Oh, it was nothing."

You affirm assertively, "I just wanted to let you know that I appreciate your work."

Here's another example: Your twelve-year-old son mows the lawn without your even asking him to do so. He comes in the house and tells you what he's done. You thank him by saying, "Thank you. That was a very helpful thing to do. I really appreciate it."

He responds aggressively, "Well, I hope you do appreciate it; it took me almost two hours!"

You affirm assertively, "I just wanted to thank you."

Receiving Compliments and Appreciation

Receiving a compliment graciously and assertively is as much a challenge as offering a compliment graciously and assertively. Some may believe that they shouldn't receive a compliment because they're not good enough. Others believe that receiving a compliment may obligate them to the one who made the compliment. But if you reject, ignore, or dodge a compliment or words of appreciation, you make it difficult for others to relate to you in a balanced and healthy manner. Receiving a compliment assertively not only affirms the recipient, but also brings a great deal of pleasure to the person who thought of the praise, considered the words, found the courage, and then gallantly offered the compliment.

Here are some guidelines for receiving compliments and appreciation assertively.

A Simple "Thank You" Will Do

When someone offers you a compliment or praise, you may respond with a simple "Thank you." You don't have to give a compliment in return or find something to praise about the other person. Accept and trust the complimenter's good intentions and enjoy the compliment.

Avoid Offending the Person Who Offers the Compliment

Few people would consciously or deliberately insult a person who offers a compliment, but people often do so inadvertently. For example, a friend says, "I like your suit. It looks good on you." In response,

Don't Say: "It's only an old suit that I've had for years."

Do Say: "Thanks. I'm glad you like it."

The Don't Say response not only causes you to miss an opportunity to say thank you and denies you the chance to feel good about this compliment, but also indirectly implies that the other person doesn't have good taste in clothing. The Do Say response offers the other person an indirect compliment that implies, "The fact that you like my suit is important to me."

Be Aware of Nonverbal Messages

Assertively respond to caring acts by establishing eye contact and speaking distinctly. For example, you've been ill and have missed work for two weeks. During this time a coworker has taken over many of your responsibilities so that you aren't too far behind in your work when you return. He does this freely without anyone's asking him. You want to thank him.

Response (passive): Drop your eyes and say, "You know you didn't have to do this," or become embarrassed and verbally stumble around saying, "Well . . . I . . . guess you . . . oh, you know what I mean!"

Response (aggressive): "What did you do all my work for? You hoping to get my job someday?"

Response (assertive): "I want you to know that I really appreciate the fact that you helped me so much at work while I was sick. That was very generous of you. Thank you."

While you may struggle to offer and receive compliments and appreciation assertively, when it comes to sharing praise and appreciation, Jesus set a fine example. In Mark 12:28–34 (NIV), Jesus is confronted by a teacher of the law. Mark's account mentions the mutual admiration of Jesus and the leader, noting that the teacher was initially impressed with the answers he heard from Jesus in that debate in the synagogue. As the leader expressed his admiration and asked his own question of Jesus, Jesus in turn commended the leader for his reply. In his usual honest, forthright manner, Jesus observed that the leader was "'not far from the kingdom of God,'" surely a radical observation given the circumstance.

At other times and in other places, Jesus drew attention to the faith of people who were not Jews to highlight the fact that the good news of salvation was for all people, Jew and Gentile alike. Jesus' lavish praise of the centurion's faith is recorded in Matthew 8:5–8, 10 (NIV):

> When Jesus had entered Capernaum, a centurion came to him, asking for help. "Lord," he said, my servant lies at home paralyzed and in terrible suffering."

> Jesus said to him, "I will go and heal him."

> The centurion replied, "Lord, I do not deserve to have you come under my roof. But just say the word and my servant will be healed. . . ."

> When Jesus heard this, he was astonished and said to those following him, "I tell you the truth, I have not found anyone in Israel with such great faith."

In Matthew 15:21–28 (NIV), Matthew makes a point of telling the reader that the Canaanite woman was not of the Jewish faith, but that she steadfastly believed that Jesus could drive the demon out of her daughter. When the disciples urged him to send her away, Jesus tested her faith and then drew attention to the tenacity of her faith with these words: "'Woman, you have great faith! Your request is granted.'" He then healed her daughter.

When Jesus was invited to have dinner with a Pharisee, he went to the Pharisee's house and reclined at the table. Luke records the rest of the story:

> When a woman who had lived a sinful life in that town learned that Jesus was eating at the Pharisee's house, she brought an alabaster jar of perfume, and as she stood behind him at his feet weeping, she began to wet his feet with her tears. Then she wiped

them with her hair, kissed them and poured perfume on them. . . .

Then [Jesus] turned toward the woman and said to Simon, "Do you see this woman? I came into your house. You did not give me any water for my feet, but she wet my feet with her tears and wiped them with her hair. You did not give me a kiss, but this woman, from the time I entered, has not stopped kissing my feet. You did not put oil on my head, but she has poured perfume on my feet. Therefore, I tell you, her many sins have been forgiven—for she loved much" (Luke 7:37–38, 44–47 NIV).

Jesus expressed appreciation for the love of this penitent woman and drew attention to her repentant and thankful spirit as well as her sacrificial gifts of perfume and devotion. Jesus wasn't reluctant to praise, compliment, and spotlight the courageous faith of the people he served. Indeed, Jesus was courageous when he offered praise in such a generally hostile environment in which church leaders were determined to find fault with him. Jesus' courage can be an incentive and an example as you resolve to compliment and appreciate those with whom you live and work.

15

Expressing and Receiving Affection

When he was a young boy, the great painter Benjamin West decided to paint a picture of his sister one day while his mother was not at home. He got out the bottles of ink and started, but soon had made an awful mess. His mother eventually returned and saw the mess. Instead of scolding him, she picked up the portrait and declared, "What a beautiful picture of your sister!" Then she kissed him. Later in life he said, "With that kiss I became a painter."

Benjamin West's mother had a choice when she returned home to find Benjamin at work—she could focus on the mess he had made or on the young artist. Her quick decision to focus on her son instead of the mess helped to shape her son's life and work. This mother's combination of affection and appreciation proved to be a powerful influence for the young artist.

Expressing Affection

Assertively offering and receiving compliments and appreciation may be difficult; expressing and receiving affection may be even more so. When you offer compliments, you're offering your best evaluative judgment as well as your personal appreciation. The risk escalates sharply, however, when you want to express feelings as profoundly personal as affection for another person.

Most people can remember sharing warm personal feelings with another person. Sometimes those feelings were happily received; probably sometimes the other person didn't respond to the expression of feeling. Remembered hurts emphasize the risks of expressing affection. On the other hand, the memories of affection gladly received give people courage to risk sharing affection again.

Here are some guidelines for expressing affection assertively.

Do Express Affection

Don't assume that others will just know about your affection for them and that you don't have to tell them. Avoid the mistake of the man who said to his wife, "Why are you angry that I never tell you I love you? I told you I loved you twenty-five years ago when we got married. If anything changes, I'll let you know!"

People sometimes take their most precious relationships for granted, spending little time to deliberately nurture and strengthen the bond. Expressing affection requires a conscious and intentional decision, especially with people who are a part of your daily life.

For example, a close friend of yours is moving to another state next week. You've been friends for a long time, and you realize that you've never really told your friend how much you've enjoyed the friendship over the years. You visit your friend. While sitting on the patio, both of you reminisce about the past and chat about the upcoming move. You want to express your feelings of happiness and satisfaction over your friendship.

Response (passive): Keep your feelings inside and instead talk only about the various arrangements being made for the move.

Response (aggressive): Joke about your feelings and act as if you really don't care that your friend is leaving.

Response (assertive): "We've been friends a long time, and I'm going to miss you when you move. I'm really glad that you're my friend."

The passive and aggressive expressions leave much unsaid and are open to personal and perhaps painful interpretation. The assertive response is simple and straightforward and leaves no doubt about the feeling intended.

Distinguish between Friendship Affection and Romantic Affection

Each person has many ways to express affection, using one style to express affection for a friend and another style to express romantic affection. You also distinguish between the way you express affection to children—your own and other people's children—and the way you express affection and friendship to neighbors, to a favorite coworker, or to a member of your church. Learning to be deliberate and assertive about expressing affection will necessarily involve learning to identify the various kinds of affection you have for people and then thoughtfully choosing the most appropriate expression.

Express Affection Directly

While a certain amount of good-natured teasing and "picking on" people is usually interpreted as a sign of good will and affection, using that particular style consistently and exclusively will make it difficult for people to understand what you really want to communicate. For example, your in-laws have come to town for a visit. You consider yourself very fortunate to have these people for your in-laws. Over the years since you've been married, they've been very supportive and accepting. When you first got married, you were worried about having conflicts with them. Instead of conflict, however, you've found love and friendship. You want to assertively express your love and appreciation to your in-laws.

Response (passive): Don't say anything and just hope that they can tell how much you care for them by the way you act.

Response (aggressive): Tell in-law jokes and then assure them that you aren't referring to them because you really like them.

Response (assertive): "I want you both to know how much I love and appreciate you. I often think of how kind and accepting you've been toward me, and I'm very grateful to you. You really are like second parents to me, and I love you."

Choose Appropriate Nonverbal Expressions

Touching is one of the most powerful ways to express affection. Some cultures have formalized the expression of good will in the form of a handshake. Other cultures forbid touching unless the people involved are very familiar with each other. Touching is a very sensitive topic for many people. When in doubt, and if your basic instinct about the situation and the person involved gives you pause about touching, don't touch. Wait for some clear indication that touching won't be offensive before initiating a hug or some other physical expression of affection. Remember that genuine assertiveness involves respect for both the affection-giver and the affection-receiver.

When expressing affection, use assertive nonverbal behavior: good eye contact, purposeful gestures rather than fumbling or fidgeting, and erect posture. When you offer an expression of affection to another person, your nonverbal behavior should support the sincerity and honesty of your words.

Express Affection in Writing

Occasionally you'll have the opportunity to express affection in writing. You might purchase a greeting card or write a short informal note that expresses your feelings about someone. You might clip a newspaper article of interest to the person or point out a television program that he or she may not have noticed. Writing your affection not only gives you a chance to individualize and personalize what you say, but it also provides a more permanent and lasting expression.

Receiving Affection

Jesus gratefully received the affectionate expression of Mary's love when she anointed him at Bethany. Martha was busy serving dinner and Lazarus was reclining at the table, as was the custom of the day. John recounts the event:

> Then Mary took about a pint of pure nard, an expensive perfume; she poured it on Jesus' feet and wiped his feet with her hair. And the house was filled with the fragrance of the perfume.
>
> But one of his disciples, Judas Iscariot, who was later to betray him, objected, "Why wasn't this perfume sold and the money given to the poor? It was worth a year's wages." He did not say this because he cared about the poor but because he was a thief; as keeper of the money bag, he used to help himself to what was put into it.
>
> "Leave her alone," Jesus replied. "It was intended that she should save this perfume for the day of my burial. You will always have the poor among you, but you will not always have me" (John 12:3–8 NIV).

Jesus understood Mary's need to express her devotion and affection in such an extravagant manner. When Judas objected, Jesus defended her action. Jesus graciously and assertively received Mary's affection, honoring her and allowing her to express her commitment to him.

Here are some guidelines for receiving affection assertively.

Decide to Receive Affection

Deciding to receive an expression of affection is an assertive act. You can decide to set aside thoughts of whether or not you deserve the affection and simply receive and enjoy it.

Sometimes receiving an expression of affection might be inconvenient, as when a young child wants you to drop everything and receive a hug or a gift, listen to a song, or observe a new skill. You may assertively decide to set aside your rights at that moment in order to accept a gift that someone who loves you wants to give.

A Simple "Thank You" Will Suffice

When someone shares affection with you, you don't have to respond with affection in return. If someone says, "I love you," you don't have to respond in kind. "Thank you" can be a genuinely assertive response that honors the other person and his or her expression of affection. A thank-you response accepts the offered affection gratefully and respectfully. You don't have to match the other person's level of affection or commitment if you don't feel that level of affection and commitment.

A very shy person might be tempted to ignore an expression of affection because of embarrassment or a fear of not knowing the right response. Once again, a simple "Thank you" is really all that's needed. Ignoring or pretending not to hear a person who is expressing affection is passive and can come across as disrespectful.

Avoid Exaggerating the Importance of the Expression of Affection

You don't need to analyze every expression of affection for hidden motives or messages, and not every expression of affection implies a lifelong commitment to a continuing relationship. Graciously accept the expression of affection and enjoy the fact that someone cares for you. The implications and full meaning of the sharing of affection will probably become clear over a period of time. In the meantime, get on with life and resolve to appropriately share affection with those you choose.

Because you can't assume that others will somehow intuitively understand your affection and caring for them, you need to learn to express and receive affection assertively. Express such feelings in easily understood terms, with sincere words and nonverbal messages that reinforce and support what you say. When you express genuine feelings of affection and caring, your relationships can deepen and grow. And when you receive such genuine feelings of affection graciously and assertively, both parties experience the benefits of encouragement and support.

PART FIVE

The Assertive, Loving Christian

16

The Assertive Choice of Passive or Aggressive Behavior

When you understand what assertiveness is and when and how to be assertive, you can also assertively choose when and how you will not be assertive. Choosing not to be assertive is an assertive decision. At times choosing passive or aggressive behavior is appropriate.

The straightforward, honest energy of assertive behavior often lends strength and security to relationships. But thoughtfully chosen passive behavior can also have a place in relationships because passive behavior can preserve a relationship or protect you from serious harm or loss. On rare occasions, aggressive behavior might be the most appropriate choice, especially when you need to give a strong "stop" message and your previous attempts to deliver that message assertively have failed.

When you possess assertion skills, you are able to make a deliberate choice about whether to behave assertively, passively, or aggressively. Knowing how to behave assertively allows you to be intentional about your own behavior rather than having the situation dictate how you'll behave. You can be proactive rather than reactive.

Assertively Choosing Passive Behavior

From time to time, Jesus assertively chose passive behavior as he lived out his life and ministry. When his message was rejected in one village, Jesus and his disciples moved on to another. When Lazarus was sick, Jesus delayed until

Lazarus died. Jesus assertively chose not to resist when he was betrayed, arrested in the garden, put on trial, and mocked by his captors. And, in an intriguing story in Matthew 17:24–27, Jesus assertively chose not to give offense but rather to pay the unfair and arbitrary temple tax imposed by Jewish leaders.

In modern times, Martin Luther King Jr. chose passive behavior in order to make an assertive statement about equal treatment under the law. Nonviolent resistance is sometimes called passive resistance because such behavior passively makes a very powerful, assertive statement.

Here are some situations in which you may choose not to behave assertively, but passively.

The Other Person Is Already Apologizing

When a person is already apologizing for something he or she did, you may choose not to assert yourself. Asserting yourself to object to the behavior is probably unnecessary and might be interpreted as "rubbing it in." While it's wise to avoid overemphasizing or belaboring the fact that the other person's behavior was offensive to you, you may legitimately mention the hurt or inconvenience his or her actions caused. In a sense, you are agreeing with the person who is apologizing, because he or she already acknowledges having done something unpleasant. You obviously have no need to ask for an apology.

You also have an opportunity to receive the apology assertively as you let the other person know that you hear and accept his or her apology. For example, you agreed to meet your friend Abby at an outdoor art fair on what turned out to be a very hot summer day. Abby was 35 minutes late and, because there were no phones available at the park, you waited in the heat and didn't even know if she was coming. You were preparing to leave the agreed-upon meeting place when Abby arrived, breathless from running from the parking area and very apologetic.

Abby: "I am so sorry to be late! I feel awful that you waited so long in all this heat. I left too late and didn't plan for the traffic. There's no excuse for it. I'm sorry!"

You: "You're right, the heat has been awful and I've been hot and miserable for more than a half hour waiting for you. I was beginning to wonder if you were coming at all. Thanks for telling me what happened. Now, come on, and I'll show you where the lemonade stand is—looks like we both could use a big, cold drink."

It Would Seriously Hurt the Other Person

You may choose not to assert yourself when it would be hurtful to another. For instance, when you're aware that a person is going through a life crisis, such as the death of a spouse, the loss of a job, or the illness of a family member, you may choose not to assert yourself regarding an issue. You might decide to delay the discussion until a later time when that person will be better able to listen and respond to you.

For example, Scott borrowed $200 from you last year, and the two of you agreed that he would repay the loan starting on September 1. On August 15, Scott was laid off after previously being assured that his job was secure. At first Scott was in shock, but now he is working very hard to find a new job; he's very worried about how he'll make his mortgage payments. You decide to approach Scott assertively and suggest that the two of you agree to a new payback date after he has a steady job.

You might also choose not to behave assertively with people who are senile or clinically depressed. Of course, if you are being manipulated and abused by such people, you may decide that it would be better to assert yourself and risk their hurt and confusion than to behave passively and thereby encourage the manipulative and abusive behavior that would ultimately hurt them as well as you.

It Would Put Your Life in Danger

You will probably choose not to behave assertively when behaving assertively would put your life in danger. For example, if you are being robbed at gunpoint, insisting on your rights and running the risk of being shot would be reckless. Choosing passive behavior in this situation is acting assertively and intelligently.

The same is true if you are with someone who is violently angry; it might be best to avoid a confrontation with that person until the heat of anger has cooled and more rational conversation is possible.

Other Personal Loss May Occur

You may also choose not to assert yourself when the dangers are not life-threatening. For example, if you think that what you assertively say or do will cost you your job and you really need to keep that job, you may choose not to behave assertively. Before deciding how you will act, consider what may happen if you do assert yourself, as well as what may happen if you don't.

In a high-risk situation such as your job, you may want to examine other avenues for self-assertion such as assertively working through the established grievance system or assertively bringing specific suggestions for change to those with authority. You may assertively choose to behave passively in one arena while assertively choosing to be active in another.

Assertively Choosing to Behave Aggressively

In rare instances, Christians may need to choose aggressive behavior. In those situations, aggressive behavior is employed only as an "I win, you lose" approach, as when Jesus cleansed the temple of money changers and merchants in John 2:13–17. Jesus' deliberate choice of aggressive behavior was free of the abuse, disrespect, sarcasm and other hurtful characteristics of impulsive aggression. An "I win, you lose" approach is by definition inflexible and single-minded, and Jesus left room for neither discussion nor negotiation as he fashioned a whip out of cords and drove them all out of the temple. Love for both the money changers and their customers fired Jesus' determination to win that confrontation.

Here are some situations in which you might assertively choose aggressive behavior.

When You Need to Send a No-Nonsense "Stop" Message

You may assertively choose aggressive behavior when you need to send a no-nonsense "stop" message and previous assertive attempts to convey limits to the offender have failed. A person who persists in physically, emotionally, sexually, or verbally abusive behavior after you've assertively objected may need to hear a no-nonsense "stop" message that is aggressive in its "I win, you lose" tone and style.

When You Need to Limit an Offender's Rights

When a person engages in illegal or abusive behavior and refuses to heed your requests to stop, you may need to make such a strong assertion and clear demand that you close off further discussion and negotiation. While assertive behavior generally honors and respects another person's rights, carefully chosen aggressive behavior limits the offender's rights when exercising those rights brings or threatens serious harm to others. You may limit a person's basic right to swing a fist if it threatens your nose or someone else's. You may refuse to give car keys to someone who is too drunk to drive.

When a Person Engages in Self-Destructive Behaviors

In addition to protecting others from an offender's dangerous behavior, aggressive behavior may be necessary to protect a person from harming himself or herself. If a person is threatening suicide or is engaged in other self-destructive behaviors such as glue sniffing, drug abuse, or alcohol abuse, you may help by delivering an aggressive "stop" message that is so firm and so definite that it cannot be ignored.

The presence of love and loving concern distinguishes aggressive behaviors assertively and proactively chosen from impulsive and thoughtless aggression. Love for the other person motivates the action, and love is the source of the courage that it takes to choose to respond aggressively to someone's self-destructive behaviors.

Assertively choosing passive behavior may be the right course for you in some situations. Respect for yourself and others will determine your choice. Assertively choosing aggressive behavior is a risky and uncomfortable act for most people. Knowing assertion skills and using those skills consistently and regularly (when problems may be more easily addressed) can make the need for assertive, respectful aggression a rare occurrence. In both instances—assertive passive behavior and assertive aggressive behavior—your guiding principle will be love, and Jesus' example will be your model.

17

Prepare to Behave Assertively

Assertive behavior is learned behavior, and you can change your behavior if you want to do so. Passive and aggressive behaviors are also learned behaviors, and you can also change those behaviors if you want to do so.

Many people apprehensively resist change because they fear the unknown or because they know they'll feel uncomfortable when they try to change long-standing patterns of behavior.

The process of giving up old behaviors and taking on new is both simple and complex. It's simple because to make a change you must simply make a change. It's complex because making even the smallest change requires you to adjust your thinking, shift attitudes, and be willing to make deliberate choices and then act on them. But this simple truth remains: If nothing changes, nothing changes. No matter how much you learn about assertiveness, you still will not become more assertive until you make a decision, gather up your courage, and finally act assertively.

How can you help yourself move along the road to change—and do it in a way that feels relatively safe and reasonable and that will actually deliver you to the moment of change with courage and enthusiasm? Here are some suggestions for preparing to behave assertively.

Prayerfully Offer Your Assertion Skills to God

Ask God to use what you know about assertiveness to help you to serve people, to build your self-respect, and to increase your skills and your willingness to show respect for others. Offer your knowledge of assertiveness to God to use in ways that will help you to encourage and support others, enhance and deepen friendships, and restore mutual respect to broken or damaged relationships. Ask God to govern your use of assertion skills so that your behavior will bring honor to God and to the whole Body of Christ.

Catch Yourself When You Go Too Far

If you have regularly chosen passive behaviors, you may need to work especially hard to establish new assertive behaviors. Your momentum may sometimes carry you over the line into aggressiveness.

Be ready to apologize assertively and learn from your mistakes when you step over the line into aggressiveness. But don't let such mistakes keep you from working toward more assertive living and relating.

Focus on Observing Behavior

Many of the situations in which you habitually behave passively or aggressively occur repeatedly. These recurrent situations provide an opportunity to observe your own behavior and to ask questions such as: What do I usually do in this situation? What would I like to change about what I do? How would I like to behave in the future?

Avoid asking yourself "why" questions because why questions invite you to speculate about motives and tempt you to try to read other people's minds. Focus on behavior rather than motives. Ask factual questions that deal with your own and others' behavior. Those factual questions will produce more useful information on which to base decisions than speculation about motives would.

You may also find it useful to use appendix A, the Assertiveness Inventory, to identify for yourself situations in which you habitually behave passively, aggressively, or assertively.

Imagine New Approaches to Old, Unsatisfactory Situations

As you observe your own and others' behavior, let yourself imagine how things might be different if you change what you habitually do in a situation. For example, if you frequently find yourself in the position of wanting to offer a compliment to someone but instead behave passively and seldom actually deliver the compliment, you may help yourself get ready for the next opportunity by mentally picturing yourself approaching the person, briefly and assertively offering the compliment, and then assertively replying to that person's response to your compliment.

Imagine some answers to these questions: What would happen if you broke an old pattern and behaved in a new way? How would your assertive behavior improve the situation? Envision a new approach to an old situation and then make some decisions about what you'll do next time.

As you envision and plan, take care to choose behaviors and make plans that are consistent with your personal style. The self-respect inherent in assertive behavior encourages you to develop your own original and uniquely personal style of applying assertive principles.

Practice, Practice, Practice

Researchers who study adult learning patterns report that active practice is the single most important factor in making lasting behavior changes. When you've decided what you'd like to do next time in a familiar but unsatisfactory situation, you might want to use one or more of these techniques for active learning:

1. Write out a script that includes the words frequently used by the other person as well as your own new, assertive responses. Think carefully about your goal for the exchange, and let your script reflect what you want to say. Recognize that the script is only a guide-

line, because neither you nor the other person will use the exact words you have written.

2. Use an audiotape recorder and keep practicing with it until you sound the way you want to sound.

3. Rehearse in front of a mirror and pay attention to non-verbal messages. Experiment with new words, new gestures, and good eye contact until you've found the style that is just right for you.

4. Use a home video camera to record your new behavior and evaluate both verbal and nonverbal messages.

5. Ask a friend to role-play with you and give you specific feedback.

Think of other ways to actively practice assertive behavior and speech. Several shorter practice sessions spread over days and weeks work better than a crash course in which you try to do too much under a lot of pressure.

Active practice also has the advantage of helping overcome *cognitive dissonance,* that uncomfortable feeling people often have when they understand and know something in their heads, but their feelings haven't yet caught up with their heads. Your feelings may be tied to old beliefs and old reasons for making decisions, so active practice can help you work with new ideas, new beliefs, and new decisions until your feelings catch up with your knowledge and understanding. For example, during active practice you may experience the uncomfortable feelings of guilt, embarrassment, or fear, or that nagging sense that "this just isn't me." You can learn to put those feelings to rest by reminding yourself that assertive behavior is God-pleasing behavior and that a certain amount of discomfort is to be expected when a person learns new skills and tries to change old unproductive behaviors. Cognitive dissonance gradually lessens as you practice new behaviors and feel more at home with your new skills. Persevere!

Involve Other People

Making changes in the way you relate to other people doesn't have to be a solitary activity. Inviting others to accompany you on your journey toward change may be as simple as deciding to tell your friends and family that you've thought about the way you usually do things and have decided you want to make some changes. You don't need to sound threatening or ominous; just make a simple, kind, assertive statement that lets others know you want to make some changes in the way you behave. If people know in advance that you'll be making changes that are important to you, they're more likely to be supportive and helpful than if they're surprised and confused by your new behavior.

You may want to share more specific goals and plans for change with a few special people, however, and ask them for feedback from time to time. You'll probably engender more support for and less resistance to your efforts if you share in advance some specific idea of what you're trying to accomplish with the changes you propose. If you invite people to be on the team with you, you might be pleasantly surprised at the support and encouragement you receive.

Identify Assertive Models

Perhaps you know someone who rather consistently behaves assertively. Most people have some individuals in their lives who behave assertively, who are able to express affection and offer sincere compliments with ease. Perhaps you've watched someone return defective merchandise in an admirably assertive manner, or you've admired someone who agreed or disagreed assertively and respectfully during a meeting. Identify those people, and carefully observe their behavior. You can learn much from role models.

Evaluate Your Assertive Behavior

Resist the temptation to focus exclusively on results.

Results are certainly important, but it's also useful to pay attention to the process of becoming more assertive. These evaluative questions may be helpful:

How did you look? Direct eye contact. Erect, confident posture. No excessive or unrelated hand and body movements. Appropriate distance.

What did you say? Comments concise, to the point, appropriately assertive. Comments definite and firm. Perhaps a factual reason, but no long-winded explanations, excuses or apologetic behavior. Message was focused and did not get sidetracked.

When did you say it? If possible, almost immediately after the other person spoke.

How did you say it? No nervous laughing or joking. No whining, pleading, sarcasm, or inappropriate apology. Firm, unhesitating voice.

As you evaluate, pay attention to your strengths and what you did well. Give yourself a pat on the back for any part of the whole you think went well. Build on those strengths and successes for the next time. No one gets it all right the first time. Ever.

Be Patient and Forgiving with Yourself

People who study personal habits and the process of changing habits say that some habits can be changed almost immediately, while others take years to change. When you're working to change from habitually passive or aggressive behavior to more assertive behavior, however, the first three weeks will be very important.

During the first two weeks, you are on fire with enthusiasm and hope. Energy runs high and the possibilities seem endless. Nothing is too difficult for you.

But by the third week, you may start fighting with yourself about the new behavior. You might think: "It's too hard to do things a new way," or "I'm really tired of working on this," or "This probably won't make any difference, anyway." Energy for change drains away, and it's tempting to go back to the old familiar behavior, even if you already know it's counterproductive.

But if you can get past that third week, you've won. You'll learn to balance hope and reality, live comfortably with a bit of internal tension, and rejoice when you realize some small victories because of your efforts to behave more assertively. After the third week, you have enough practical experience to begin to form and act on more realistic, workable goals. Be patient and persistent.

In the process, be kind to yourself. Focus on what you did well and accept as a challenge for the next time any part that didn't go as you would have liked. Change is hard work, so give yourself encouragement along the way.

18

A Large Bag of Gold Coins

A story tells of a poor, old farmer who uncovered a large bag of gold coins while plowing a field with his old mule. He carried the bag of gold into his barn, sat down on a milking stool, and began to think about what all that money could do for him.

He thought to himself, "If I buy a tractor, my neighbors might wonder where I got the money or they would want to borrow the tractor. Maybe my wife would want half. With that kind of money, she'd leave this old farm and me for sure. If my kids find out about it, they'll fight with one another over it just like they fought over the mashed potatoes when they lived at home. I don't think I could handle all of that. It's better if things don't change." He took one gold coin and put it in his pocket and threw the rest into the well.

He then walked into his house and said to his wife, who was busy darning socks, "Look what I found in the field— somebody must have dropped it there years ago." His wife looked up and exclaimed, "The Lord was looking over you today and blessed you!"

The farmer was afraid of the changes his new wealth might make in his life. "It's better if things don't change," he thought. And while it was certainly possible that things might have changed for the better, he was still unwilling to take the risk. So he gave in to his fear and turned his treasure over to dark imaginings of gossiping neighbors, bickering children, and a greedy and faithless wife.

It was the farmer's wife, however, who recognized the blessing in even one gold coin. Had the farmer recognized his golden treasure as a blessing from God, he might have thought of ways to use it for the glory of God. He might have sat on that milking stool singing hymns and praises to God.

He might have imagined food for the hungry, help for the poor, and financial security for himself and his wife in their old age.

Your new understanding of assertiveness is your treasure. You can sit on your milking stool and imagine dark consequences—the alienation of friends, the rejection of family, the wagging tongues of critics. Or you can recognize assertiveness as a skill that can be used by God for the good of all—enhanced relationships with friends, renewed respect in your family, God-pleasing self-esteem for yourself, and an emerging confidence as you reach out in Christian love to people you've never met.

You can keep your golden treasure stored in some dark well within you and use but a fraction of its wealth, one gold coin of many. Or you can offer to God what you know and understand about assertiveness and ask God to help you use fully the entire abundance of riches.

Your new understanding of assertiveness is your treasure. Sit down on your milking stool and imagine great things for yourself, for the good of your neighbor, for the glory of God. And may the people who share your treasure exclaim, "The Lord was looking over us today and blessed us!"

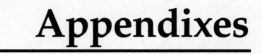

Appendixes

Appendix A
Assertiveness Inventory

Everyone behaves passively, assertively, or aggressively at some times and in some situations. This inventory will help you determine those situations in which you're most likely to be passive, aggressive, or assertive.

Instructions

The following questions will help you assess your preferred style in certain situations. Be honest in your responses since anything less is self-defeating and pointless and will distort your results. Circle the letter of the statement that describes you best.

1. When someone expresses a belief, an idea, or an opinion, I:
   a. feel inhibited about expressing my own
   b. respect the belief and feel comfortable expressing my own
   c. defend my belief but downplay the other person's

2. When someone takes my place in line, I:
   a. allow it, say nothing, and feel helpless
   b. believe I have a responsibility to respect my rights, respect the other person but not the behavior, and take steps to correct the situation
   c. resort immediately to angry, guilt-inducing words

3. In social situations, I:
   a. try to become invisible, avoid talking to people, or try to stay clear of situations where I might be embarrassed
   b. usually feel valued, respected, and self-confident; mingle freely

     c. control and monopolize conversations; some-
times speak tactlessly

4. Under stressful conditions, I am prone to:
   a. feel helpless, overwhelmed, anxious, paralyzed
   b. recognize my stress level, identify what is creating
   the stress, and deal with it
   c. become irritated and annoyed

5. When a salesperson tries to sell me merchandise I
   don't want, I:
   a. find it hard or impossible to say no
   b. am straightforward and appropriately honest and
   feel comfortable saying no
   c. become hostile and insulting and slam the door

6. When a clerk says, "Who's next?" and a person who
   arrived after me says, "I am," I:
   a. say nothing and feel inwardly angry and ignored
   b. point out the error tactfully by saying, "I believe I
   am next"
   c. tell the people around me how unfairly I have
   been treated and walk out

7. In a discussion or debate, I:
   a. am reluctant to speak up or may begin statements
   with "I'm sorry"
   b. respond openly and honestly to what is said
   c. think I have to have the only right answer

8. If a person has borrowed something of value and is
   late in returning it, I:
   a. feel inwardly angry, but say nothing or apologize
   for asking for its return
   b. mention that it's overdue and that I'd like it back
   c. demand its return with threats about what I will
   do if it isn't returned

9. During an argument, after the other person has had enough, I:
    a. give up and apologize guiltily for displeasing or making the other person feel uncomfortable
    b. agree to discuss the issue at a later date to clarify the rights, issues, or needs through negotiation
    c. continue to pursue it

10. When expressing my feelings, I:
    a. become inhibited about expressing them, or begin by saying, "This may be dumb, . . ." or "I'm sorry, but . . ."
    b. generally feel self-confident, valued, respected; use "I feel . . ."
    c. insist that my feelings are all-important; do not respect the feelings of others

11. When someone watches me while I work and I feel uncomfortable and distracted, I:
    a. say nothing; become anxious and nervous
    b. ask the person to stop
    c. become defensive and hostile, and ask the person to leave

12. When a person in authority deals unfairly with me, I:
    a. feel helpless and say nothing
    b. feel confident in my position and calmly call it to his or her attention
    c. immediately start an argument and insist on my rights

13. If someone near me in a movie is loudly chewing and popping bubble gum, I:
    a. try to ignore it, yet feel inwardly annoyed
    b. ask the person to stop
    c. slightly raise my voice and tell my friends how annoying the person's behavior is

14. When talking to a person, I:
    a. find it difficult or impossible to make eye contact
    b. look directly at the other person
    c. stare forcefully until the other looks away

15. When my restaurant meal is improperly prepared or served, I:
    a. say nothing, eat it anyway, and hope someone else speaks up
    b. ask the server to correct the situation
    c. embarrass the server and threaten not to return

16. I usually deal with my own anger by:
    a. saying nothing, feeling guilty and then depressed
    b. maintaining my dignity, respecting others but not their behavior and using "I" messages
    c. losing my temper and raising my voice

17. I express love and affection by:
    a. putting myself down, feeling unworthy and unlovable
    b. showing warmth and closeness openly and honestly
    c. seeking to meet only my own needs, demanding love or affection from others

18. Concerning the dividing of household chores, I:
    a. apologize for asking for help and feel I'm stuck with the work he or she won't do
    b. work with others to negotiate a mutually acceptable agreement
    c. let unexpressed feelings build up inside and then blow up

19. When my new toaster doesn't work, I:
    a. keep it or ask someone to return it for me
    b. return it and ask for a replacement
    c. return it but become loud, angry, and demanding

20. When I need small favors or help from family or friends, I:
    a. say "I'm sorry, but . . ." or "I hate to ask, but . . ."
    b. ask freely, understanding that others may say no
    c. demand what I want, implying they owe it to me

21. When a favorite relative expresses a viewpoint different from mine on a controversial issue, I:
    a. immediately assume I am wrong and back down
    b. speak openly and honestly and respect the other's view
    c. protect myself; tactlessly tell the other that he or she is wrong; use my words in an accusative manner

22. When someone makes an unreasonable request of me, I:
    a. fill the request but feel helpless and manipulated
    b. refuse respectfully or negotiate the request
    c. believe my rights have been violated and refuse the request with offensive or guilt-inducing statements

23. If I am disturbed by someone's smoking near me, I:
    a. believe I have no right to tell the person I am bothered
    b. tell the person I am bothered by the smoke
    c. with irritation and annoyance, noisily move away

24. To get others to do something, I:
    a. say nothing, hope they will offer to do it on their own
    b. make a request
    c. try to get them to do what I want by using sneaky or manipulative methods

25. When my landlord or a worker needs to make repairs or finish a job, I:
    a. make it myself or don't ask and live with it as it is

b. calmly ask that he or she do whatever is his or her responsibility
c. become sarcastic, threaten, or call names

Additional Instructions

Go back over the inventory and mark a *P* next to every question for which you chose an *a* response. The *a* responses are passive responses.

Mark an *A* next to every question for which you chose a *b* response. The *b* responses are assertive responses.

Mark an *AG* next to every question for which you chose a *c* response. The *c* responses are aggressive responses.

When you have marked all your responses, review the results. What are the kinds of situations most likely to call out a passive response in you? An aggressive response? An assertive response?

Appendix B
Basic Human Rights

We are created in God's image—so Genesis 1:27 tells us, and we believe it. We are loved by God—so John 3:16 tells us, and we believe it. There are no distinctions to be made among us—so Galatians 3:28 tells us, and we believe it. We are priests, all of us, a royal priesthood—so 1 Peter 2:9 tells us, and we believe it. These are the good earth from which our basic human rights spring.

- Each person has the right to be treated respectfully.

- Each person has the right to say no without explanation and without guilt.

- Each person has the right to slow down and take time to think.

- Each person has the right to change his or her mind.

- Each person has the right to ask for what he or she wants.

- Each person has the right to ask for information.

- Each person has the right to make mistakes.

- Each person has the right to make choices and accept the consequences of those choices.

- Each person has the right to own and express his or her own feelings.

- Each person has the right to ask for help.

- Each person has the right to maintain a separate self that is accountable to God and independent of the expectations, the approval, or the influence of others.

A Great Follow-up to *Speaking the Truth in Love*

Caring Criticism: Building Bridges Instead of Walls

William Diehm, a retired minister and psychologist, explores what he calls "the greatest battle of my life" and "the number one problem [of] people who come to see me for counseling"—how to give and receive criticism.

Everyone faces the challenge of coping with criticism from others—and it can be especially difficult for pastors and church leaders. Effective leaders also must master the art of correcting people without hurting them or making them angry.

Dr. Diehm draws on his 50 years of experience as a Christian counselor and provides practical illustrations from daily life. With a gentle style, he shows readers how to give non-threatening, helpful criticism and how to respond to criticism in positive ways.

With its exploration of how to break down walls of defensiveness and build bridges of caring, assertive communication, this book is a great follow-up to *Speaking the Truth in Love.*

To learn more about *Caring Criticism* or to order copies, log on to www.stephenministries.org or call Stephen Ministries at (314) 428-2600.

Two Ministry Systems from Stephen Ministries®

The Stephen Series

 The Stephen Series is a complete system for training and organizing laypeople to provide one-to-one Christian care in and around their congregations.

Stephen Leaders—pastors, staff, or lay leaders—are trained to begin and lead Stephen Ministry in the congregation. Stephen Leaders, in turn, equip and supervise a team of Stephen Ministers, congregation members who provide ongoing care and support to people experiencing grief, divorce, hospitalization, terminal illness, unemployment, loneliness, and other life difficulties. As a result:

- hurting people receive quality care during times of need;

- laypeople use their gifts in meaningful ministry;

- pastors no longer are expected to personally provide all the care that people need; and

- the congregation grows as a more caring community.

More than 10,000 congregations and other organizations from more than 150 denominations—and from across the United States, Canada, and 24 other countries—are enrolled in the Stephen Series.

Koinonia Leadership

Koinonia Leadership is a system of whole-congregation leadership that empowers a
Christ-centered, mission-driven team to lead the congregation in a new and powerful way.

The purpose of Koinonia Leadership is to help congregations identify and overcome challenges, recognize and capitalize on ministry opportunities, and become more and more what God wants them to be.

A congregation's Koinonia Leadership Team is composed of five to ten carefully selected leaders—including the pastor, perhaps other church staff, and several laypeople—who receive practical, in-depth training in how to lead *together*.

Koinonia Leadership will benefit:

- declining congregations (revitalization);

- plateaued congregations (vitalization); and

- growing congregations (previtalization).

Koinonia Leadership can help *any* congregation become stronger and healthier—increasing its ability to grow disciples, transfom lives, make a difference in the community, and carry out Christ's mission.

To learn more about the Stephen Series or Koinonia Leadership, contact:

Stephen Ministries
2045 Innerbelt Business Center Drive
St. Louis, Missouri 63114
(314) 428-2600
www.stephenministries.org

Two Resources to Help Those Who Are Hurting

Journeying through Grief

Journeying through Grief is a set of four short books to give or send to a grieving person at four crucial times during the difficult first year after a loss:

1. *A Time to Grieve,* at three weeks after the loss
2. *Experiencing Grief,* at three months after the loss
3. *Finding Hope and Healing,* at six months after the loss
4. *Rebuilding and Remembering,* at eleven months after the loss

Each book focuses on the feelings and issues the person is likely to be experiencing at that point in grief, providing encouragement, hope, and the assurance of Christ's presence. Written in a warm, friendly style, *Journeying through Grief* provides a simple yet powerful way to show continued care and support to those who are grieving.

Many pastors and congregations use the books as part of their grief ministry. Individuals can also use *Journeying through Grief* as a way to reach out to friends, neighbors, coworkers, or relatives who experience a loss.

Each set of books comes with four mailing envelopes and a tracking card that makes it easy to know when to send each book. Also available is a *Giver's Guide* containing suggestions for using the books as well as sample letters to personalize, adapt, and include with each book.

Don't Sing Songs to a Heavy Heart: How to Relate to Those Who Are Suffering

Pastors, lay caregivers, and suffering people alike have high praise for *Don't Sing Songs to a Heavy Heart* by Dr. Kenneth C. Haugk, a warm and practical resource for what to do and say to hurting people in times of need. Forged in the crucible of Dr. Haugk's own suffering and grief, *Don't Sing Songs to a Heavy Heart* draws from his personal experience and from extensive research with more than 4,000 others who have experienced suffering.

For anyone who has ever felt helpless in the face of another person's suffering, *Don't Sing Songs to a Heavy Heart* offers practical guidance and common-sense suggestions for how to care in ways that hurting people welcome—while avoiding the pitfalls that can add to their pain. Combining sound psychology and solid biblical truth with deep personal experience of pain, grief, and care, this book will touch caregivers' hearts and help them find the words and actions to bring God's presence and care to hurting people.

For more information or to order copies of *Journeying through Grief* or *Don't Sing Songs to a Heavy Heart,* log on to www.stephenministries.org/care or call Stephen Ministries at (314) 428-2600.

Ministry Courses from Stephen Ministries

Discovering God's Vision for Your Life: You and Your Spiritual Gifts

Resources to motivate and mobilize members for meaningful ministry

 This complete set of integrated resources provides congregations with an effective way to help members discover their spiritual gifts and become involved in gifts-related ministry. The centerpiece of these resources is a gifts discovery course that helps people understand their own spiritual gifts, gives them a solid foundation in the theology of Christian ministry and discipleship, and motivates them to use their spiritual gifts in service to others.

Christian Caregiving—a Way of Life

The definitive approach to distinctively Christian care

Built around the best-selling book *Christian Caregiving—a Way of Life*, this course helps congregations teach their members the basics of distinctively Christian caring and relating. Participants grow in their ability to care for one another as  they learn how to pray with someone, share from the Bible during a caring conversation, speak words of forgiveness, and much more.

Caring Evangelism: How to Live and Share Christ's Love

Evangelism training for people who never thought they could be evangelists

This course turns the book *Me, an Evangelist? Every Christian's Guide to Caring Evangelism* into a learning experience that helps Christians share their faith with others naturally and comfortably. As participants grow spiritually, they are equipped to show Christ's love in their daily lives by words and actions that others welcome. Using this course on a regular basis can enrich your congregation's spiritual growth, evangelism training, and outreach efforts.

Caring for Inactive Members: How to Make God's House a Home

A caring response to hurt and alienation

This course takes the anxiety out of ministering to inactive members by equipping participants to relate confidently and effectively to those who are separated or alienated from the church community. Inactive member ministry doesn't have to fall solely on the pastor. Church staff, lay leaders, and congregation members can use these resources to address the issues that can cause inactivity and to care for inactive members, welcoming them back into God's house.

Antagonists in the Church: How to Identify and Deal with Destructive Conflict

A ministry-saving resource for pastors and lay leaders

Pastors, governing boards, and others will find the practical methods offered by this book and study guide helpful in identifying and dealing with church members who attack leaders and destroy ministry—as well as in creating a congregation environment that prevents future attacks.

For more information about these ministry courses, contact:

2045 Innerbelt Business Center Drive
St. Louis, Missouri 63114
(314) 428-2600

You can also log on to www.stephenministries.org to learn about or order these and many other resources from Stephen Ministries.